MAGIC MOTORS 1930

A Marmon publicity photo taken at the the Oakland, California, airport on February 28, 1930.

MAGIC MOTORS 1930

BROOKS T. BRIERLEY

GARRETT AND STRINGER, INC.
PUBLISHERS • COCONUT GROVE

 Published in the United States of America by Garrett and Stringer, Inc., Coconut Grove, Florida.

Distributed by Howell Press, Inc., 1147 River Road, Suite 2, Charlottesville, Virginia 22901.

Inquiries regarding this book should be addressed to Brooks T. Brierley, Garrett and Stringer, Inc., P.O. Box 330697, Coconut Grove, Florida 33233-0697.

Duotone printing in Hong Kong.

Library of Congress Cataloging-in-Publication Data

Brierley, Brooks T.
Magic motors 1930 / Brooks T. Brierley.
p. cm.
Includes bibliographical references and index.
ISBN 0-9615791-2-9
1. Automobiles—United States—History. 2. Automobiles—United States—Pictorial works. 3. Automobile industry and trade—United States—History. I. Title.
TL23.B6524 1996
629.222'0973'09043—dc20 96-35110
CIP

Contents

Introduction

This began as a sequel to *Auburn, Reo, Franklin and Pierce-Arrow versus Cadillac, Chrysler, Lincoln and Packard.* That book covered the time period from 1927 to 1934; here, it is 1930 to 1942. Quickly changing product and market circumstances during the first four years of the 1930s make them some of the most fascinating years in automotive history, so this book takes a second look at that period. *Magic Motors 1930* provides new discoveries of information and photographs, and completes the story of the automotive industry's reluctant metamorphosis.

Magic Motors 1930 is not meant to be a comprehensive marque-by-marque history. Rather, it emphasizes some specific points of history in detail, adding period photographs to provide an authentic setting for the cars. I have assumed that the reader has some knowledge of this subject and have done away with the introductory formalities, delving right into this era's fascinating details. The California luxury car dealers, a look at *The New Yorker*'s automotive reporting of the time, important business points of each marque, the drama in each marque's state-by-state registrations, and some overseas sale registrations: all contribute evidence of the magic and reality of what was happening in the 1930s—these magnificent motor cars were going out of style.

This book owes much to the help of others. I would like to thank those who contributed the information and photographs that are presented here: Gene Babow, Fern Beattie, Tom Behring, Stuart Blond, Albert Boosing, Gregg Buttermore, Bob Casey, John Conde, Robert Conte, Bill Creteur, Robert Denham, Peggy Wise Dray, Peggy Dusman, Dan Erickson, Maria Eymann, Barbara Fronczak, Barbara Gifford, Chris Gill, Roger Gloor, Ron Grantz, Louis Helverson, Franklin Hershey, Tom Hubbard, Herb Jorgensen, Dean Krimmel, Cathleen Latendresse, Brita Mack, Skip Marketti, Mary Markey, Keith Marvin, Jean Moulin, Francis Owens, Mark Patrick, George Norman Pierce III, Ron Redelli, Cynthia Reed-Miller, Don Richetti, Jerry Riegel, Janet Ross, Stan Smith, Thomas Solley, Lynda Springate, Susan Sutton, Dace Taube, Jennifer Watts, Pat Wellington, Dale Wells, Elizabeth Wolfe, and Waite Worden.

(opposite) A Series 81 Pierce-Arrow has pulled to the side of the road in the hills above Oakland, California, in 1928. The French coachbuilder, Saoutchik, dressed up Series 81 production bodies with extra chrome and three-tone paint. But he could not camouflage a wonderful but now-outdated automotive concept of hand-hammered aluminum bodies powered by a six cylinder engine.

At the end of 1928 Duesenberg introduced its new supercar for the 1930s, the Model J. This Holbrook-bodied limousine was one of six series custom designs available. Only two were built. This car was retrofitted with the now trademark radiator shutters.

Overview

"Our volume this year is not so great," lamented E. W. Headington, the fellow in charge of Stutz's New York City showroom in the Ritz Tower, to a *New York Times* reporter in March 1930. The October 1929 stock market crash, euphemistically described elsewhere in the *Times* as "recent unpleasantness," had begun to affect people's lives. But Headington's complaint was also about the accelerating consolidation of America's luxury automobile manufacturers. Together these two forces were reducing Stutz's 1930 New York sales volume 76% from 1929, an unusually high percentage. Stutz's first reaction was to raise the price per car by an average of $300—a fair sum of money then—to maintain profits.

Both Packard and Cadillac shared some of Stutz's sales problems. Packard's 1930 American registrations were off 36% from their 1929 peak; Cadillac's off a bit less, 20%. But for 1930 Cadillac introduced a spectacular new model with a sixteen cylinder engine, making it the cynosure of motordom. Lincoln was also having sales problems, attributable to a stagnant product. Registrations for 1930 were down 29% from 1929 (which were off a further 20% from 1926).

On the West Side of town, in the heart of automobile row at Broadway and 57th Street, Pierce-Arrow's first quarter 1930 sales set records. A completely redesigned line with a powerful eight cylinder engine, introduced for the 1929 model year, was still enticing buyers a year later with its combination of mechanical sparkle and exclusive lineage. Nearby, at Broadway and 63rd Street, Peerless was shedding the least expensive part of its line to rebuild cachet. Unfortunately, its sales declined under the weight of the additional influence). At Franklin, also nearby at Broadway and Columbus Circle, sales were not a problem at all. Indeed, the sales resurgence at Franklin and Pierce-Arrow in 1929 and 1930 temporarily reversed the sales trend that had favored Detroit-built luxury cars. But, a sorcerer's apprentice situation existed at the Franklin factory—several thousand Franklins were made in excess of sales in 1929 and they had to be sold in 1930.

None of this post stock market crash mentality took away from the forthcoming Automobile Salon, the annual exhibit of custom-built automobiles held in New York, Chicago, Los Angeles, and San Francisco. *New York Times* Salon "observer" Elizabeth Onativia described that year's Salon in an analogy that saw the automobile industry as an army and the Salon cars as the army's leaders: the cars were "very handsome Generals, with here and there a Major, on parade." (Onativia gave no clues as to which cars only ranked as Major). The timing of the first two Salons, Chicago and New York, in early and late November respectively, further expressed the importance of what was taking place: a full month before the regular automobile shows, the Salon allowed the (supposedly) most prosperous customers to buy the best cars first.

The 1930 Salon showing the 1931 models was only slightly less grand than that of 1929: 90 cars versus just over 100. As might be expected, the most popular luxury automobile, Packard, had the greatest number of chassis in the show (14). For the first time Packard had its own custom coachwork, in addition to the coachbuilder-designed models. Cadillac and Lincoln each showed twelve cars—all the Cadillacs were assembled by their in-house coachbuilders, Fleetwood and Fisher; all the Lincoln bodies were by independent coachbuilders. There were eight Rolls-Royces, all with Brewster (their in-house coachbuilder) bodies, six Pierce-Arrows, seven Franklins, eight Duesenbergs, plus smaller numbers of other marques such as Cunningham and Cord. The Marmon Sixteen was new at the Salon, showing off its LeBaron-bodied production models. However, reports of the show pointed out it would not be in production until early 1931. A new duPont model, the H, with a wheelbase of 145 inches (unexpectedly adapted from the old Stearns-Knight chassis) was shown with a berline body by Merrimac. It was very different from the sporty image usually associated with duPonts but reflected good demographics since the limousine buyer was the one luxury car customer still buying.

Chrome replaced color as the point of interest in these 1931 cars. Metal tire covers were preferred over cloth. As always, there was a long list of fine details to notice, such as the crotch mahogany woodwork (taken from the roots of the tree, it had a distinct, uneven grain) in a Cunningham convertible, and the cast aluminum dash in all twelve duPont body styles.

The bottom line on all this was that reported actual sales for the Chicago Salon (perhaps a public relations gesture) exceeded the previous year's level, a considerable accomplishment. But the absence of Ruxton, Locomobile, and Stearns-Knight, and the coachwork of recently defunct Holbrook and Floyd Derham from the Salon was an ominous indication of what was about to happen.

THE LAST AUTOMOBILE SALON

Changes in the organization of the Salon of 1932 models unwittingly conspired with the Depression to end the Salon. The show reverted to opening in New York, and with only about half the cars (50) of the 1931 model Salon. Chicago's Salon, previously held in early November, was moved after New York's, which held its Salon at the very end of November/beginning of December. This meant winter weather replaced the milder fall weather of the previous Chicago Salons and, consequently, attendance dropped (a significant factor, as Chicago typically sold the majority of cars in the four Salon exhibits). Equally important was the report that Packard would not exhibit, confining its displays to special showings in two of its New York showrooms.

Nevertheless, advance publicity for the Salon's coming West took place on schedule. One of the Duesenbergs to be exhibited was shown in *The San Francisco Chronicle*. Then the show's organization fell apart. *The Los Angeles Times* finessed the issue with the headline, "Auto Salon Conducted At Biltmore," followed by the sub-heading explaining, "Latest Model Lincolns To Be Viewed This Week." It was described as a combination automobile show and

The last New York City Automobile Salon was held in the ballroom of the Commodore Hotel starting November 30, 1931. The Depression notwithstanding, it was still a dazzling display of vehicles.

Two Duesenbergs fill the bottom right of the photograph, while a German Maybach extends from the left corner. Behind the Maybach are four Belgian Minervas. In the center are various Lincolns. A Brewster-bodied Springfield Rolls-Royce coupe in a teardrop shape is at the back of the room.

When the Commodore Hotel (now the Grand Hyatt) was built in the late 1920s, it became the site of the Salon because a large freight elevator served the ballroom. But it was a logistical nightmare exhibiting cars in the hotel's lobby—they had to be taken by hand down the grand staircase.

Salon, with Lincoln's original set of Johannsen measurement gauges vying for attention among the fifteen custom bodies on display. Still, all was not bad news: Brunn's Double Entrée coupe, with doors that could be opened at the front or rear, had been sold in New York. A second model had to be built for the Los Angeles Salon and was sold there (despite such "demand," no additional copies were made).

After Los Angeles, the Lincoln Salon went to San Francisco at the beginning of March 1932. This last Salon was the most visually impressive. It was held in one of the most beautiful indoor spaces in the world: the garden court of the Palace Hotel, a glass-domed room hung with crystal chandeliers (preserved today as it was then). Still, one of the two San Francisco newspapers simply ignored the show. The Salon was over. No one but Lincoln would continue the show after its disappointing results in the East.

Lincoln records have yet to reveal how this was done. Edsel Ford's interest in coachbuilding suggests his letters and wires (as might be expected of someone with his tastes, his telegrams were sent by the Mackay System rather than by Western Union) would reveal something, but they do not. Even so, accessible correspondence of the time—from independent and manufacturer's coachbuilders, a factory sales branch, and one of the customers—provides the background for the end of the Salon.

For example, on May 3, 1932, Edsel Ford described to coachbuilder Hermann Brunn his pleasure with his new Brunn-bodied phaeton, finished in several shades of gray metal, fabric, and leather (gray was Ford's favorite color). The following week Brunn wrote back, starting with the expected thanks, adding, "whenever we do anything for you, we always put everything we have on the ball." Two paragraphs down Brunn declared: "It is to be regretted that owing to conditions, the organization which built your phaeton is slowly slipping away from us. In fact, if it were not for the order you gave us last summer, we would have long since closed our doors. My only reason for telling you this, is that we want you to know that we appreciate your courage in ordering a few bodies when nobody else would do so."

At about the same time, duPont's New York City distributor, former Mercer and Duesenberg salesman A. J. Miranda, Jr., made a special report to his four other stockholders. E. Paul duPont, the president of duPont Motors, was among them. The undated five-page memorandum began: "I am extremely sorry to have to inform you that because of prevailing conditions and lack of operating capital our Company cannot possibly continue in business." Miranda cited the lack of a new model as one of the reasons for poor sales; "the interest in, and the demand for duPont cars, has dwindled to practically nothing."

The duPont distributorship had begun in 1928 with great promise. A striking showroom, fitted out as an Art Deco foyer, was leased in the Delmonico Hotel at 522 Park Avenue. Although duPont production rose from 54 cars in 1927 to 84 in 1929, the car did not catch on in New York. Agencies for Delage and Maybach were added to broaden the sales base. By 1932 the six demonstrator cars in stock were readied for sale as part of winding up the business.

The distributorship's last public hurrah was a full-page ad in the March and May issues of *Fortune* (then the leading magazine for automobile advertising).

LeBaron continued its coachbuilding business through the Depression as a subsidiary of mass body builder Briggs Manufacturing Company. Ralph Roberts, LeBaron's salesman, adapted to the new situation by becoming a Briggs man. His letter to Edsel Ford in March 1932 reflected someone at the peak of his profession. "Peering into the future, projecting future trends," he began, "we have drawn our conception of the possible car of tomorrow." A model was included in the package, which Roberts described as "a streamlined form . . . with very simplified system of manufacture." Aware that Ford did not like to be too far ahead of the times, Roberts raised the issue and at the same time offered a solution. "At first blush our design may look too un-conventional to you. We would like to have you set it up somewhere in your office where it can 'season' in your estimation for a week or so." A reply acknowledging receipt did not come from Ford's secretary until early May. Did Roberts make the sale? Automotive historians will recognize this scenario as the first step in the development of the Lincoln Zephyr.

The band still played on for one Willoughby customer, wintering at the National Hotel in Havana, Cuba. In January 1933 he was exchanging airmail letters with the Lincoln factory (the series custom buyer did not deal directly with the coachbuilder, but with the chassis manufacturer's factory representative) to finalize the building of his limousine, which was to be delivered to Holland that spring. Against the background of popular resentment then building against coachbuilt automobiles (in New York City people on relief threw stones at cars coming out of Rollston's shop) that would eventually end their production, the correspondence reveals the many details needed to complete a custom order: the cost of the chauffeur's request for a Yale lock on the gas cap to match the lock on the hood, the pressure required to turn the window "regulator," and the size of the owner's initials on the door (to be half again as large as the type of his letter). The most important point to many coachbuilt customers, including this one, was the feel of the seats. The owner's acceptance of the seats, the "cushion fitting" in the parlance of custom body procedures, could be more important than the look of the car. Here, the customer noted he had tried a number of car seats and, having described the qualities of seat depth, pitch, etc. he wanted, pointed out that they were not available in other Willoughby bodies he had tried but in only one of Lincoln's standard factory-bodied limousines.

As the customer finished his last letter, he mentioned that he was about to continue traveling to California by ship. Contact by return mail was not assured. His instructions added, "always to the Empire Trust Company, 580 Fifth Avenue." The Empire Trust Company survived the March 1933 bank holiday. The customer left Cuba just before a revolution overthrew the government. So it would appear that this transaction was completed as originally intended.

Former President Herbert Hoover (seated, in the left foreground) was the guest of honor at the opening of the Oakland, California, Bay Bridge in November 1936. Packard's California distributor, Earle C. Anthony, to the right of Hoover, provided the 1936 Packard twelve cylinder convertible sedan for the occasion. A 1932 Lincoln follows.

This bridge and San Francisco's Golden Gate were the culmination of years of lobbying by California automobile dealers. Don Lee, the Cadillac distributor, was actively involved also, but did not live to see these projects completed. Anthony's ingenuity represented Lee in the Cadillac radiator cap ornament on the Packard.

California

New York may have been the center of automobile sales (and Michigan, of course, the base for much of its production) but California was its showplace. The state, then and now, mirrored events in the industry and exercised a trend-setting influence on automobiles. One clue to California's importance was its coachbuilders' creativity. In the motor car's first years, vehicles sold in California were often modified to that region's unique demands and tastes with specially built tops and bodies painted and trimmed in interesting ways. The results were so attractive that these features were demanded throughout the country. The focal point for this customization was the multi-dealership distributors, some with an in-house coachbuilding staff. Each distributor made a contribution.

WALTER MURPHY

Walter Murphy was a member of a Michigan oil and timber family who came West to seek another fortune. His father was an investor with Henry Leland, so he easily became Lincoln's first California distributor. The Lincoln factory was not interested in adapting its homely cars to the California market, so Murphy started his own coachbuilding shop, buying out New York City's Healey & Co. and moving some of its equipment and employees to Pasadena. When Henry Ford bought Lincoln in 1922, Murphy changed to representing Hudson. The coachbuilding shops fostered series custom Hudsons, but now emphasized work on other chassis, as only so much coachwork could be done on a nonluxury marque. With a stable of talented designers—Franklin Hershey and Phil Wright on the smart side and Wellington Everett Miller doing more conservative things—Murphy set a simple, dramatic style with a high quality of execution. Angelenos, as Los Angeles people are called, took pride in Murphy's worldwide reputation, pointing out that an English Rolls-Royce was shipped all the way from "dear ole Lunnon" for their expertise. (It is hard to picture today, but coachbuilding was just a business at the time. One former Murphy employee recently recalled that Walter Murphy did not come out to the Pasadena plant to visit or meet for business or admire the cars. He stayed at headquarters in Los Angeles.)

The apogee of Walter M. Murphy Motor Company was reached as 1929 turned to 1930. The business, including an agency for Curtiss airplanes, employed 600 people. A new main showroom was completed in Los Angeles at the corner of Ellsworth and Flower. The grand opening in January 1930 was Hollywood's equivalent (including the eventual ruin of the host) of the party that minister Fouquet gave at Vaux-Le-Vicomte for the King of France. So many people came it was hailed in newspapers as Hollywood's "social center for day." Alice White, a sex symbol at the beginning of talking pictures, dedicated the building; vaudeville actor Frank Fay was master of ceremonies. A fashion show modeling designs from 1st National Pictures (now Warner

Brothers) was included with feature numbers from the popular musical *Hit the Deck*. A roomful of stars (Murphy's wife, Marion Coakley, an actress, brought him into the movie colony)—Mary Eaton of Ziegfeld Follies fame, Loretta Young, Wheeler and Woolsey (a comedy team), Lilyan Tashman, and Edmund Lowe among them—were present.

Hudson was hit very hard by both the Depression and competition from new makes such as DeSoto and Viking. California registrations for 1930 were only one-third of 1929. Some coachbuilding business was lost when Murphy's shop superintendent, J. Gerald Kirchoff, set up his own shop in Pasadena. So there wasn't much positive to say about Walter Murphy's business in 1930 save his being the second most highly insured Angeleno at $1,732,500 (Gloria Swanson was first at $2,000,000), no doubt a function of key person insurance required by his bankers. Then there were signs of trouble. In 1931 Murphy transferred his Hollywood branch at 6250 Hollywood Boulevard, across the street from Pantages/Graumann's Chinese theater, to his right-hand man, Richard Carlson. Murphy's name was publicized for supporting William Randolph Hearst's plan for a five-billion-dollar national prosperity loan to help the country overcome the Depression. In 1933 a modest single-column article in the *Los Angeles Examiner* announced "Murphy, Car Dealer, Asks Bankruptcy." His liabilities were listed as seven times his assets. The coachbuilding shops were taken over by two employees who gave it their names, Bohman and Schwartz. With the Hudson distributorship assumed by Earle C. Anthony, Murphy went to work in the oil business.

JOHN LUTHER MADDUX

Maddux, Inc. was Murphy's successor as Lincoln distributor. Founder Jack Maddux is perhaps better known for his Maddux system, a West Coast combination of planes and Sante Fe and Pennsylvania railroad land-and-air service backed by high-profile investors such as Cecil B. DeMille. Charles Lindbergh flew the airline's inaugural flight, then worked for the airline in a technical capacity that included development of its own airplane. When Lindbergh was out West he would be Maddux's houseguest, an event that was reported in newspapers 3,000 miles away in New York.

A native of Alabama who moved to California, Maddux began his business career as an automobile salesman who took airplane rides on his time off. During World War I he looked in a third direction, by joining the submarine service. Taking over the Lincoln distributorship in 1922 soon led to acquiring the first Ford Trimotor airplane for his new Maddux Airlines. In the summer of 1937, Maddux sold his Lincoln distributorship to concentrate his business energies on licensing and promoting an electric-magnetic brake for automobiles. Two weeks after his 49th birthday that July, he was dead of a heart attack.

RALPH HAMLIN

A racing car driver known for establishing records between various Pacific Coast points, Ralph Hamlin became Franklin's California distributor in 1905. Franklin's reputation as a durable, reliable car was offset by its odd styling, "a freakish appearance" by one account. Style's importance in the early 1920s clashed

This is the Maddux, Inc. Beverly Hills service department in 1930. The roadside service truck created from one of the cars was a feature offered by many luxury marques in the area.

with Franklin's engineering-led design philosophy, jeopardizing California sales. Hamlin led a dealer revolt with an ultimatum to the factory: redesign the car to more conventional tastes or they would give up selling it. A prototype design contest ensued, with Hamlin having Walter Murphy develop one sedan and the Franklin factory hiring J. Frank deCausse, who had done landmark design work at Locomobile, to do another. The deCausse proposal was adopted and Franklin continued through the 1920s as a thing of beauty. However, available sales data show no discernable change in registations due to the car's redesign.

A savvy businessman, Hamlin managed to remain in business throughout the Depression. When Franklin took its new V-12 model on a preproduction cross-country test in the winter of 1932, Hamlin saw the car and concluded that it was the wrong car for the time. Although the factory was not to be dissuaded on the V-12, it appears to have built the Reo-based Olympic middle-price model in response to his objections.

By 1933 the winding down of Franklin's business became a concern and Hamlin added Graham to his showrooms. The results are in Graham's subsequent steady California sales increases. The addition of Graham also improved showroom traffic, as Hamlin sold 79 Franklin cars in 1933 versus 75 in 1932—quite a feat with overall Franklin registrations falling by nearly half during the same period. Publicity about Hamlin's success took its toll: in the summer of 1933, he, his wife, and a maid were robbed at gunpoint in their palatial Los Angeles home. Newspaper accounts noted that the three gunmen got $10,000 in jewelry and "plunder," making their getaway by car. But they did not take any of Hamlin's personal collection of favorite Franklin cars, which he kept after the house was torn down to make way for a park in the 1950s. They remain on exhibit in Los Angeles today.

PAUL HOFFMAN

When Studebaker bought control of Pierce-Arrow in 1928, their ace Los Angeles distributor, Paul Gray Hoffman, took over selling Pierces from longtime dealer William Bush, moving the showroom from Figueroa and 21st in Los Angeles to 9628 Wilshire Boulevard in Beverly Hills. Hoffman had become Studebaker's branch manager in 1917 and bought the distributorship from Studebaker in 1925, when he was 34 years old. At the same time a dealer revolt (similar to the one at Franklin, contesting an inadequate new model) propelled him to take charge of sales for the entire Studebaker company. Hoffman introduced an open door policy to foster good dealer-factory relations and dispensed with some of the trappings of business to do so: for instance, he answered his own phone and required his associates to do the same. His credibility is still legend—"Paul Hoffman told me this, so I know it's true," a prominent educator recalled recently.

When Studebaker went bankrupt in 1933, Hoffman became one of the receivers and is credited with maintaining sales during the critical reorganization period. To finance retooling the 1934 Studebaker, Hoffman and the other receivers sold the company's interest in Pierce-Arrow. But he personally kept the Pierce-Arrow distributorship, giving the independent luxury automobile company an aggressive 18-dealer network throughout Southern California kept at Studebaker-subsidized levels.

DON LEE

Don Lee may have been the most dynamic of the California distributors. A Lansing, Michigan, native who came West to work in the lumber industry, he began selling Cadillacs during the first decade of the century, later branching into coachbuilding, radio stations (KHJ and KFRC among them), and the first regularly scheduled television station (which sent out an hour's programs between six and seven in the evening).

Lee was a driven man. The publicity from his three marriages (his name could be found in Louella Parson's newspaper column) and his various business interests record a higher profile and greater details of his person than his automotive counterparts. He took issues in public, fought a Sunday closing law, and was an avid yachtsman known for racing. His *Elia*, a 146-foot-long yacht built at the Craig shipyards in Long Beach, was purchased from George Whittel, the San Francisco man still remembered for owning six Duesenbergs. Lee's coachbuilding business was known for its advanced styling—so well appreciated that General Motors hired its stylist, Harley Earl, to start its own in-house styling group.

A spring 1928 fad among businessmen was to ask, "if I were broke, what would I do?" *The Los Angeles Examiner* asked prominent Angelenos this question in one of its columns. Lee replied with his characteristic boundless optimism. He would start again in the automobile business, taking whatever position was available: mechanic, car wash work, etc. He had no doubt, once started, he would soon be on his way back up again.

In January 1934 Lee signed his twenty-ninth and last contract with Cadillac, agreeing to sell 2,225 Cadillacs and LaSalles worth $8,000,000 (about 20% of 1934 production). Now and then, Lee retreated to the Ambassador Hotel, then a park-like resort in the center of Los Angeles, for a few days to escape the pressure and folderol of work. He was there in August 1934. During a quiet dinner with his wife and son, he collapsed and died of a heart attack. His automobile business continued and thrived under his son, who increased his $1,000,000 inheritance twelve times before his own untimely death in 1950.

EARLE C. ANTHONY

Earle C. Anthony was Packard's California distributor for an incredible 50 years, from 1906 to 1956. His involvement with the automobile began with designing and building the first car driven on the streets of Los Angeles—an electric runabout he made as a high school student in 1897. From then on he spent his life promoting use of the automobile; his accomplishments were made particularly intriguing by the mix of his electrical and mechanical engineering training and the idiosyncrasies of his personality (he founded the campus humor magazine, *The Pelican*, while at the University of California at Berkeley).

Anthony began selling Buicks. He kept the franchise after taking on Packard but was challenged by Buick's head, William Crapo Durant, to do one or the other (something that did not prevent Anthony from selling Durant cars in the early 1920s). He called a friend then running a bicycle shop, Don Lee, who took over the Buick business. Lee later swapped the Buick franchise for the Cadillac distributorship. Anthony and Lee often got together for a project. They founded the National Supply Company to sell gasoline in the first gas stations. They were called red-and-white filling stations and the personnel dressed in red, white, and blue. They used a chevron as a trademark. Standard Oil of California, their supplier, soon took notice and bought up the fast-growing chain (which had 250 outlets by World War I), taking the chevron trademark for its own.

Some of Anthony's other accomplishments were championing road building, mobilizing car dealers for such projects as San Francisco's Golden Gate Bridge, and organizing a bus line that grew into the Greyhound system. He saw to it that Packard trucks replaced the mule teams in Death Valley. Anthony brought the first neon sign to California (from France) to illuminate his gas stations on Wilshire Boulevard in Los Angeles and owned radio stations KFI and KCEA.

KFI and KCEA were Anthony's guardian angels. The stations were originally housed in the top floor of his Los Angeles headquarters; twin radio antennas sent out the broadcasts from the roof of the building. The stations thrived during the Depression and replenished the hundreds of thousands of dollars Anthony lost yearly selling Packards.

Anthony remained active until the end, concentrating his efforts in southern California, and by all accounts enjoyed every minute of it. His greatest thrill may have been in 1932 (often considered the worst year of the Depression) when he fulfilled a lifetime desire and withdrew $1,000,000 in cash from his bank. He put the money in a satchel and walked through downtown Los Angeles to his office. Six guards took the money back to the bank.

Business Points

AUBURN, CORD, AND DUESENBERG

As the Depression took hold, Auburn fought back and made a hash of it. In 1930 E. L. Cord personally developed the specifications for a new car. Posing as a prospect, he visited different automobile showrooms in the eastern United States to experience a direct feel for the market. The results of his fact-finding were Auburn's totally redesigned 1931 models: improved mechanical features such as synchromesh transmission, seductive Cord-like looks, and prices cut by a third. Sales nearly trebled over 1930. By 1932 results were back to 1930 levels, still an accomplishment. But in 1933, failure to redesign for the new streamlining trend caused sales to plummet again. Exports, once a substantial source of business, languished, aggravating the decline. Design errors limited sales of the all-new 1934 line, requiring a reworked 1935 model to be introduced just after midyear. Sales then were only marginally better.

Paralleling this were developments in the company's personalities. E. L. Cord lost his first wife in 1930 and never returned to Auburn, Indiana. Corporate headquarters became Chicago. There, he expanded an interest in aviation and put together a conglomerate holding company investing in various businesses such as Checker taxicabs and shipbuilding. When Cord delegated operating decisions to his executives, they did not always agree, aggravating the effects of his absence. (Cord was not a desk person and left the office for weeks and months at a time. He "keeps in circulation," said Auburn president Roy Faulkner.) Disagreements between Faulkner and Duesenberg head Harold Ames were said to kill the 1937 Auburn, and Fred Duesenberg's untimely death from a car accident in 1932 was a loss that may never be fully quantifiable.

Auburn's sales revived slightly through the middle of 1935, when month-to-month registration figures indicate a decision to gradually shut down. April registrations in 1934 were 373 cars, then 538 in 1935 and 278 in 1936; August 1934 saw 510 sales registered versus 415 in 1935, and 98 in 1936. American registrations mask a tremendous improvement in export sales at this time; from 314 in 1933 to 1,144 in 1934 and 1,574 in 1935. Operating losses into 1936 were substantial—the company regularly lost $500,000 or so every three months. Much of this was in heavy sales and administrative expenses—as much as one-third of sales volume, when the competition used only half that percentage. The extent to which this represented Auburn's support of related enterprises or the subsidy of company-owned dealerships (the landmark showrooms in Los Angeles, Chicago, New York, and Auburn) is unclear.

At the end of 1936 Auburn announced that its new 1937 model would not be introduced until later in 1937. Prototypes that were built indicate it was to be based on the Cord 810 body. But it was never put into production. After E. L. Cord sold his interest in the company in August 1937, it remained in vehicle manufacturing for a short time, building Stutz's Pak-Age delivery van, and then as a subcontractor on the new Jeep.

Cord's namesake automobile was a casualty of the 1931 economic crunch. The L-29 model was expected to sell 5,000 units a year. The novelty of front-wheel drive and the smashing good looks fell short of selling such a car then. It was discontinued early in 1932 amidst rumors of adding a twelve or sixteen cylinder model to the line.

The Cord was revived at the end of 1935. Newspaper reports suggest the car was first designed for the $1,000 class, but that concept was dropped with the decision to use the new Duesenberg as the Cord. The design of the new car, designated 810, was spectacular. But it was developed so quickly that it displayed its predecessor L-29's flair for imperfect mechanical innovation. By the time the bugs were worked out, demand for the 810 and its super-charged version, the 812, was halted by the sale of the company.

The Auburn Automobile Company's master-piece, the Duesenberg model J, was in a class by itself when introduced for the 1929 model year—a European supercar concept built in the United States. The J was conceived as a limited edition of 500 cars, so many of the parts, such as the frame, were all built at once and stockpiled, with the expectation of being sold in a year or so. By the end of 1930 some 350 had been built, another 50 in 1931. Duesenberg fore-saw the effects of the Depression on the J and began developing a new type of car, one that was stream-lined with a V-12 power plant. It was announced for introduction in 1934. Concurrently, from 1931 on, the company repeated its development of the J, building only a small quantity of new cars to continue interest until the replacement model was ready. Drastic reduction in production was concealed by a handful of well-publicized sales and the introduction of super-charging the J engine, the model SJ. Rebuilding and modifying existing Js became the primary factory activity.

When the all-new 1934 Auburn failed to revive that marque, introduction of the new Duesenberg was postponed. A year later it became the revival of the Cord. The J continued and was treated to some full-page advertising in magazines such as *Fortune* and *Country Life* in 1934 and 1935. Also, in 1935 a small edition of ten cars, called JN because of their modifications, was built. That November, the new V-12 Duesenberg was given a full-page advertisement in the export edition of *The American Automobile*, a trade magazine. But, at the same time, cold-blooded assessments of the Duesenberg business were made. The Philadelphia branch was closed, the last engines ordered from Lycoming. In early 1936 the factory is said to have refused an order for ten cars from the Chicago branch. Two breathtaking Rollston-bodied convertible sedans were built for the November 1936 automo-bile shows as the company's final appearance as a going concern. The official end came shortly after E. L. Cord's sale of Auburn in August 1937.

ROLLS-ROYCE AND BREWSTER

When Rolls-Royce of America took control of Brewster & Co. in 1925, it immediately stopped production of Brewster automobiles and concentrated the company's efforts on its original coachbuilding. Sales of Rolls-Royces built in Springfield, Massachusetts, never met expectations. The best year was 1929 when 350 cars were sold (with profits only slightly above $100,000). As the English company improved or introduced new models, the American company, a licensee, followed slowly because of retooling costs. The American-built Phantom I came out a full year after its English counterpart, and the improved Phantom I was never built in the U.S. In 1931 Springfield agreed to relinquish its manufacturing rights and England built 120 or so left-hand drive Phantom II chassis for Springfield to body and sell. A number of Phantom I chassis were still in stock but these were not all sold until 1935.

In 1934, as a final effort to stay in business, Rolls-Royce of America (then doing business as the Springfield Manufacturing Company) revived the Brewster automobile, not as its grand forebears, but as a modest luxury car. It was built on a stretched Ford V-8 chassis, clothed in adaptations of Brewster's magnificent Rolls-Royce coachwork. Measurements of Brewster's sales volume vary between 115 and 300 cars through 1936, when Brewster went out of business. Detailed data published in *Automotive Industries* show only 21 registrations in 1935 in New York City (15), Westchester County (3), and Long Island (3). These quantities in the company's best market suggest both small overall production and substantial non-New York sales (quite reasonable as the Ford chassis could be serviced anywhere).

The Brewster factory in Long Island City, New York, reverted to the Brewster family after the Springfield business closed. They used the enormous 400,000 square foot space to manufacture airplanes for use in the regional conflicts in Europe just prior to World War II.

The Brewster name received a well-publicized last hurrah. In 1939, winding up a transaction left over from the coachbuilding business, Brewster sued a publisher in Poughkeepsie, New York, for the $600 balance due on a $5,000 order. She had refused to pay because the body was not tall enough to accommodate a man's top hat. Brewster argued that the buyer herself had supplied the specifications for the car; it merely executed the order. The *New York Times* described the situation in an article entitled "High Hat Figures In Suit," and followed up with an editorial defending a fellow newspaper publisher. The inductively reasoned piece danced through a consideration of collapsible opera hats and the car owner's knowledge of passenger compartment heights. It read as though Eric Hatch of *Country Life*, George Sutton of *Vanity Fair*, et al—the trappings of 1920s motor journalism—had come out of hiding, a fitting end (the outcome of the suit was not published) to one of the more glamorous chapters of automobile coachbuilding and manufacture.

FRANKLIN

Franklin began 1930 with an enormous inventory problem: it produced 14,432 cars in 1929 but sold only 10,704 (a difference not explained by exports). Cutting production restored some balance to the situation, but the adjustments made to the company's profit and loss statements undermined its financial health. Once the Depression took hold in mid-1931, it would be just a few short months before the banks took control. They installed their own chief operating officer, Edwin McEwen, to run the company. McEwen had some ideas about cars and proceeded to influence Franklin automobiles. The new twelve cylinder line, just introduced at the January 1932 Automobile Show in New York, was revised to incorporate less costly conventional engineering (Franklin built a high percentage of its own components, adding to both its uniqueness and its manufacturing costs) and rebodied with handsome LeBaron designs (said to have originated as a proposal for Lincoln). To foster sales at the other end of the price spectrum, a Reo-bodied car with a Franklin engine, called the Olympic, was introduced for 1933. Between these two lines was the traditional Franklin four-fifths size luxury car, the Airman.

Edwin McEwen caught pneumonia in January 1934 and quickly died from it. Without him, and faced with continued weak demand for Franklin cars, the banks let the company go bankrupt in April. In desperation, the company's export department sought an exemption from Canadian customs' definition of a complete car by eliminating bumpers and other accessories to bring the list price of its basic sedan below $2,100, reducing the ad valorem tax from 40% to 30%. Franklin continued to offer the Olympic for sale through 1934, while there were attempts to refinance the company. Both Harry Wahl, the man who tried to revive Mercer in 1931, and E. L. Cord both tried to put deals together. The *New York Times* disclosed in December that the last step had been taken to reopen the plant, when the trustee's sale sold all the assets for $278,750 to a company called Franklin Motors Inc. Sale of the plant again in March 1936, just as the city of Syracuse was about to begin tax foreclosure, did not stop hope of restarting production. That November there was talk of reviving the company as a manufacturer of "bantam class" cars. Nothing happened.

REO

Ransom E. Olds organized his second automobile company (his first was Oldsmobile) in 1905, using his initials for its name. It prospered as a builder of both middle-price cars and trucks. Then it sought to expand its market with a glamorous line of high-price cars. The Reo Royale debuted for the 1931 model year. Offering conventional engineering, it sought distinction from the design of its bodies, a result guaranteed by selecting Amos Northup to style them. Some beautiful cars were made—as many as 1,500 or so by one estimate—from 1931 to 1934. A handful of custom and series custom models were also built, including a Dietrich-bodied close-coupled sedan with its ashtray set between the front seatbacks to foster conversation. A 153-inch wheelbase model was added to rival Duesenberg's size. The economics of this were soon challenged and the response was to discontinue the line. Reo continued with its wonderfully named Flying Cloud models into 1936, when their production became no longer feasible. Then the company began to concentrate on developing its line of trucks.

PIERCE-ARROW

Pierce-Arrow began 1930 in high gear. First quarter registrations set a record. Studebaker's not quite two-year control of the company, with its revision of the car lines and manufacturing processes, was a success. The determination to make Pierce-Arrow one of the leaders of the luxury market (as it had been before World War I) continued as the Depression began. Maintenance of factory-owned sales branches in major cities around the country cost $850,734 in 1932 alone (an amount just short of the $1,000,000 Packard was said to spend on its factory branch system). Pierce automobiles were kept current mechanically and visually—matching Cadillac's pace of yearly restylings. A special model, the Silver Arrow, built for the 1933 automobile shows, became the most important automobile of 1933. Then Studebaker went bankrupt. Within several months Studebaker sold its interest in the company to a group of enthusiastic Buffalo businessmen, eager to return a business institution to local ownership. Monthly sales rates increased later in the year and a tiny profit was recorded one quarter.

In response to deteriorating luxury car registrations (62,809 in 1930 to less than 20,000 in 1933), a new lower-price line of cars, the model 836A, was readied for the 1934 model year, together with a complete revision of its senior cars. At the same time, prices of the senior Pierces were raised $250 to make sales room for the new model. April production was increased to 400 cars to meet anticipated demand. The higher prices, together with supply shortages from an industry-wide tool and die makers' strike, stifled initial sales. Then, the 836A's pricing cannibalized demand from the senior cars. Sales for the first six months were only marginally ahead of the same period in 1933, 934 versus 902. The losses from maintaining the infrastructure inherited from the Studebaker years forced bankruptcy that summer. At that point, E. L. Cord tried to merge Pierce with Auburn, Reo, and Franklin, but no one could agree about how to do it.

With the Buffalo community continuing support, Pierce-Arrow emerged from bankruptcy in May 1935. Relieved of its factory branch burdens, it went forward at a measured pace. Its 1936 cars were redesigned and enjoyed increasing sales for the first half of the year (411 versus 375 for 1935). Later that year a line of trailers was introduced to diversify. But losses from operations continued to trouble the banks; in November 1936 regular manufacturing ceased. Only enough cars and trailers to give the appearance of a going concern would be built. An attempt to raise money to build a medium-price car à la Packard ended with the 1938 recession. That May, the possessions of the last independent non-Detroit luxury car manufacturer in the United States were sold at auction.

Still, Buffalo did not give up. The beginning of World War II created an opportunity to revive manufacturing in the Pierce-Arrow plant. Its one and a quarter million square feet of space was considered an ideal production site for the new Jeep and other wartime products. George Norman Pierce II (a civil engineer who was namesake and grandson of Pierce-Arrow's founder) flew to Buffalo from his home in Knoxville, Tennessee (at the time a trip by plane alone was a significant act), to discuss heading the new company. The effort failed. Instead, the factory's contents were sold for scrap, and Jeep bodies were built in the Auburn, Indiana, plant.

STUTZ

In 1930 Stutz's owners were negotiating a merger with St. Louis car companies Moon and Gardner, with the idea of transferring production from Indianapolis. Someone had second thoughts about this plan; suddenly, a capital contribution of nearly $2,000,000 was made (this was several months after the stock market crash) by Stutz's investor group. The money was spent revising the straight eight engine with dual overhead camshafts and four valves per cylinder, improving output to 156 HP. The new model was called DV-32 (a designation crafted to imply multicylinders) and was set off by some impressive series custom coachwork. But like some other new luxury models introduced in 1931, such as the Reo Royale and the Marmon Sixteen, it was doomed for lack of buyers.

Only a handful of Stutz cars were built in 1934. But an unusual amount of activity was left in a business that had supposedly stopped manufacturing. At the end of the year, two new lines of cars were announced for 1935, both with aerodynamic lines that had never been seen on a Stutz. But a look at the floor plan of the 1935 New York Automobile Show revealed no space reserved for them. Stutz's European popularity kept its English branch open and selling cars through 1935. There was also an attempt to diversify by building a small delivery truck called Pak-Age Car. Then, a well publicized ruckus over the sale of Stutz stock in violation of the Security Law ended plans to go forward (something losing $250,000 or so every year had not done). In April 1937 the company declared bankruptcy; one year later, in August 1938, the bankruptcy referee set the date for sale of its assets.

MARMON

Marmon diluted its prestige franchise in the late-1920s with the Little Marmon compact car, then with a medium-price line called the Roosevelt. So the company's response to the Depression was to go to the very top of the market with a line of sixteen cylinder engined cars. The cars came out for the 1931 model year, a full year after Cadillac's V-16 and at a time when the Depression held a real grip over the economy, so production was limited to 390 cars.

The concurrent failure of Marmon's less expensive eight cylinder models, despite extensive redesign to match the Sixteen's for the 1932 model year, suggests a weak dealer organization plagued the company. To continue, the company's namesake and head of engineering, Howard Marmon, designed and built a V-12 (three-fourths of the existing V-16), presumably for the 1934 model year. Marmon 1933 production was limited to 86 Sixteens, but a number of eight cylinder models continued to be sold overseas (where last year's American model often was this year's current one). The Australian state of Victoria was the company's last foreign market stronghold, still selling two or three cars a month into 1933.

Early in 1934, a new company, American Automotive Corporation, was being formed by Harry Miller (the racing car and engine manufacturer), Preston Tucker (former sales manager at Pierce-Arrow, famous in the late 1940s for his Tucker automobile), and others to resume Marmon production. It sounded promising. Miller racing engines were considered in a league with Bugatti. But nothing came of it and Stewart-Warner bought the Indianapolis factory in November 1937. A truck-building affiliate, Marmon-Herrington, formed in 1931 to make four-wheel drive commercial vehicles. It continued the Marmon name for several more decades.

PEERLESS

Peerless was a wonderful old name, known, with Packard and Pierce-Arrow, as one of "the three P's of fine motoring" before World War I. It subsequently lost interest in the luxury market and became just another above-average-price automobile during the 1920s. In 1929 new management realized the error of selling such cars under the Peerless name (things had been so good in the 1920s that the medium-price market did about the same volume as the luxury cars). Alexis de Sakhoffsky's impressive body designs were introduced. Eliminating the least expensive models aggravated sales lost from the first effects of the Depression, but Peerless still made a little money—about $67,000—in 1930.

In the summer of 1931 Peerless made conflicting moves: it announced it was joining the multicylinder race with both V-12 and V-16 models for 1932 but selling its parts business to a firm specializing in parts from defunct automobile companies. Peerless correctly read the economic crunch that fall and stopped production (three V-16 chassis had been completed) on November 4, 1931. The company had nearly $2,000,000 in the bank and began buying back stock and paying a liquidating dividend. A subsequent bankruptcy to clear the air before changing the business to brewing Carling beer was challenged in a stockholder's suit, which the company successfully defended. It thrived as a brewery and is still a textbook example of how business can adapt to changed circumstances.

RUXTON

For several months after its November 1929 debut at the Automobile Salon, the Ruxton appeared as a glamorous front-wheel drive counterpart to the Cord. An aggressive promoter, Archie Andrews, assembled the Ruxton by subcontracting various stages of manufacture to the Moon, Gardner, and Kissel factories. His disputes with Kissel forced that company to seek bankruptcy protection, which also stopped production at the other manufacturing sites. Some 500 cars are thought to have been built in the short six months or so of production.

CUNNINGHAM

Rochester, New York-built Cunningham persevered during the 1930s. It steadily lost its competitive position by failing to update the car mechanically and renew its once unique factory-built coachwork. In 1934 a new direction was taken, building town cars and close-coupled sedans on Ford V-8 chassis. That continued the cars for another two years, but without profitable results. So production was shut down, with business energies used to make such things as garden tractors and military tanks.

There were so few Cunninghams made, perhaps 100 per year at the beginning of the 1930s, that published American registrations excluded them. But the marque had a more quantifiable colonial-style following overseas: there were nearly 100 registered in

Cuba in the late 1920s, and by 1938 there would still be five in Sao Paulo, Brazil.

CHRYSLER

Chrysler began the 1930s by gearing up for a 1931 Imperial that would be both an aesthetic and mechanical tour de force. In 1934 another completely new design, the Airflow, was introduced, but the bulbous cab forward design negated the impressive engineering details of the car. Like some other automobile manufacturers, Chrysler did not make significant year-to-year changes in its cars until the late 1930s, so there was no meaningful revision in the Imperial line until 1937. Contributing was Elsie de Wolfe, the most famous interior designer of the time (known equally for styling the interiors of some Locomobiles and serving drinks at a mirrored cocktail table in the bathroom of her Paris apartment). One press report credited her with designing the entire car; a Chrysler ad touted her counseling the design and showed her signature with a handwritten "approved" to drive the point home. Why Ray Dietrich, the talented former coachbuilder who was in Chrysler's employ (and is supposed to have designed this model), did not share in this project's accolade remains an unanswered bit of automotive history.

During the mid-1930s, Philadelphia's Derham Body Company added a DeSoto dealership to its business. Together with the coachbuilder-friendly non-unitized structure of the 1937 Chrysler Imperials, this facilitated Imperial's return as a custom body showpiece, taking up where fallen marques such as Marmon, duPont, and Franklin with their Waterhouse, Murphy, and Locke bodies left off. The return was short-lived. Chrysler restyled in 1939 and again in 1940 with almost complete emphasis on its medium-price models. A prewar burst of pizzazz came in two LeBaron-bodied models, a Thunderbolt convertible and a Newport phaeton for the 1941 model year. They represented the most advanced automobile styling but they were treated as show cars from a production standpoint. Only six of each were actually built.

DUPONT

The duPont came from a picturesque factory in southeastern Pennsylvania (which, understandably, gave Wilmington, Delaware, as its home address). It made its name in the late 1920s by giving its model G cars a Jaguar-like charisma. Most parts of a duPont came from outside the factory, such as the powerful 140 HP Continental straight eight engine. But to call it an assembled car (which it technically was) is misleading. Each model was clothed in a series custom body—some merely attractive, others spectacular. A racing model, entered in contests here and in Europe, was a status symbol. Sales were centered in five factory-controlled branches in Baltimore, Boston, Philadelphia, New York, and Los Angeles. Export sales were minimal—20 cars out of the 483 produced in the firm's twelve years—but had intriguing destinations (most went to Latin America—with seven sold in Argentina and one in Costa Rica). Then, duPont production collapsed from 84 cars in 1929 to 36 cars in 1930.

The turning point for duPont's aspirations does not appear to have been the Depression so

The careful architectural style of the duPont factory in Moore, Pennsylvania (near the Delaware border), reflected the image of the car. It remains intact today, down to the trademarks carved into the corner peaks of the building.

This photograph was taken in 1925. DuPont cars of that year had yet to blossom into their high-style heyday.

much as persistent management problems in its Los Angeles branch. What should have been one of its best markets became its most disappointing. "The California Situation," as E. Paul duPont, the company's president, called it, ended when the showroom lease was allowed to expire at the end of 1930. In February 1931 the branch's inventory of 16 cars—a black and red roadster, an orange and black "special" sedan, a four-passenger blue speedster, etc.—was put on a steamship and sent back to Philadelphia.

Some additional changes were made in 1933. The lights stayed on in the company's main showroom in Philadelphia's Bellevue-Stratford Hotel as duPont Motors was quietly absorbed into the duPont-controlled Indian Motocycle Company. The company's trademark is said to be still maintained by descendants of duPont's owners.

LINCOLN

The Lincoln of 1930 was not a great deal different mechanically than the Lincoln of 1923, a function of founder Henry Leland's engineering skills and Henry Ford's reluctance to change. Edsel Ford's management of Lincoln gentrified it by applying Ford mass production concepts to the coachbuilt car: offering small lots (20 or 50 or 100) of a specially-designed body, i.e., the series custom. A trend began in doing so and Lincoln quickly became a popular luxury marque. By the late 1920s flawless style and manufacturing perfection alone did not sell luxury automobiles. Lincoln, which Ford brought from nowhere to third place in luxury car sales by the mid-1920s, was passed in sales by Pierce-Arrow and Franklin as well as Cadillac and Packard.

When the time came to revise the Lincoln, the result would be a product of a tug-of-war between the manufacturing processes of Henry Ford (and his head of operations, Charles Sorensen) and Edsel Ford's interest in the craft of automobile production. The first revision, called the model K and introduced for the 1931 model year, was overdue. A twelve cylinder K, the KB, was introduced in 1932, a year when multicylinder engines were introduced throughout the industry. But the use of important engineering details—independent front suspension, hydraulic valve lifters, and the like—were resisted or prohibited. Yet the breathtaking coachwork continued: a dazzling variety of body styles supplied by a number of different coachbuilders.

Stories of Edsel Ford's guiding Lincoln give short shrift to his understanding of the automobile as a mechanical object. Detailed studies reveal that Henry Ford instilled a mechanical inquisitiveness in his son and that, among other things, they both shared a passionate interest in building and driving racing cars. Edsel Ford's best manufacturing example of this was his development of the Lincoln Zephyr.

Lincoln prices were in the middle to upper end of the luxury market. When it came time to build a medium-price version, the Zephyr, similar parameters were targeted. The new model was a bit grander than the Packard 120, had dramatic contemporary styling, and was powered by a V-12 engine (based on the Ford V-8) rather than the 120's eight.

Lincoln's line of big cars sold in increasingly smaller quantities as each year of the Depression passed: 1,515 in 1936, 977 in 1937, 416 in 1938, and 133 in 1939. Nevertheless, Edsel Ford planned an entire new line of these cars for the 1941 model year. A full-size clay model was built. With the success of the Continental about to be enjoyed and a major revision to the Zephyr series in place for 1940, a third new line of cars at this time would have placed enormous pressure on Cadillac's lead in the prestige market—enough, perhaps, to snatch away its recently won position. It was a very good strategic move, never made because of the elder Ford's increasing resistance to his son's ideas. So the third line never reached production.

PACKARD

At the end of the 1920s Packard's research and development work on a new model centered on a prototype in-line twelve cylinder engine packaged in a Dietrich-designed silver and orange convertible coupe body. The company was uncertain what to do with it, so the car spent the summer of 1929 with one of the Packard family, elegantly wandering around northern Michigan. When fall and the 1930 automobile shows came, the car and Packard faced a new production model sixteen cylinder Cadillac offered in dozens of body styles. Assorted other challenges included the revival of Peerless, Stutz, and Pierce-Arrow; luxury models from middle-price manufacturers Elcar and Jordan; and new front-drive marques from Ruxton and Cord.

Packard's lead in luxury registrations was so great—triple Cadillac's 1930 numbers—that its position, both in the United States and abroad (where it had a large following), was not immediately threatened. It had an unusually harmonious and effective system of dealers and distributors (a number factory-owned), which provided Packard with the equivalent of the top J. D. Powers customer satisfaction rating of the day. Then, a series of product errors—late (1932) introduction of a multicylinder model, poor pricing of the new Light Eight model in 1932 (it was not priced low enough to attract new buyers, so it only lured purchasers away from the more expensive models), and failure to adapt contemporary streamlining in its 1934 cars—steadily eroded its position.

Packard correctly anticipated the permanent shrinking of the luxury car market and threw its weight into developing a new $1,000 medium-price car, the model 120. By 1934 half the plant had been gutted for it; General Motors men had been brought in to design, build, and sell it. Introduced for the 1935 model year, the 120 was an immediate sales and financial success. The concept did so well that a second, even cheaper ($800) six cylinder model, the 110, was brought out in 1937, saturating the market. There was a business cost in doing this: the luxury Packard relinquished its sales lead to Cadillac in 1936, but Chryslerization (i.e., selling cars in several price classes under one name) was the price paid to stay in the automobile business.

By 1938 the big Packards were showing signs of neglect when the expatriate American coachbuilder, Howard "Dutch" Darrin, returned from Paris to set up shop in Hollywood, California. Actor Dick Powell, a Packard enthusiast, wanted a special convertible-bodied car. What Darrin designed for him was coincidentally to be Packard's answer to the Lincoln Continental. The factory then had a hundred or so built for several years as a series custom. This convertible victoria led to Darrin's helping Packard fashion a new model—the extraordinarily handsome Clipper sedan. Packard's change in product direction (giving up production of the twelve cylinder line in 1939) limited the Clipper to a visual phenomenon rather than an engineering accomplishment. Even so, it allowed the company to begin the 1940s with the expectation of continuing a good show.

BUICK

Buick was a dynamic automobile company in the 1930s. It had demonstrated upscale aspirations in the 1920s—its radiator shell often suggested Packard's—which were effectively advanced by its head, Harlow Curtice. Sharing some body shells and components with Cadillac/LaSalle gave the top Buick line the materials to work with. Coachbuilders began to use the Buick chassis, both in the United States and Europe. The Duke of Windsor, when King Edward VIII of England, used a factory-built (Canadian) Buick town car rather than the expected Daimler. At the end of the 1930s the Buick series 90 line took the final step in motordom and ordered a series of Brunn-bodied cars for the 1941 model year. It was too much a threat to Cadillac. Under pressure from GM management, all four models in the series were withdrawn and Buick was put forever in the shadow of Cadillac's luxury.

CADILLAC AND LASALLE

The 1930s were Cadillac's time. It thrust itself to the forefront of the luxury market, introducing a sixteen cylinder-engined line for the 1930 model year. No one but Marmon had a multicylinder response before 1932, giving Cadillac two precious years with a unique product. When demand for luxury cars began to turn from noticeable presence to modesty in 1933, Cadillac and its sister LaSalle continued to lead with annual styling changes and engineering advances such as independent front suspension—features many competitors could no longer afford to offer. Packard's 1935 introduction of a medium-price car under its own name (LaSalle took on this task for Cadillac), gave Cadillac the final push to the top. It became the best-selling American luxury car in 1936 and has stayed there ever since. (In 1937, to make sure Packard would not recapture the lead, Cadillac doubled its advertising budget.)

At the same time, charisma simmered behind the scenes at LaSalle. Auburn's designer, Al Leamy, went to work in the General Motors central styling studio after the 1934 Auburn failed. Auburn's fizz began to rub off: at least two supercharged speedster proposals (neither Leamy's) were drawn. Neither appears to have been built. Cadillac then concentrated on putting sizzle into more standard models such as the Series Sixty Special, an owner driven close-coupled sedan with striking lines (a decided contrast to Packard and Lincoln's emphasis on coachbuilt models). Also introduced in 1938, perhaps as insurance against the revival of Packard, was a new short stroke V-16 engine. This top-of-the-line model was quickly withdrawn at the end of 1939 as competitive pressures melted away: Packard announced the cessation of its twelve cylinder cars in late 1939, at the same time the demise of the big Lincoln K models became certain. The luxury car battle was won—against both the independent manufacturers and the other glamorous Detroit marques.

Sales Registrations

State-by-state sales registrations from 1930 to 1936 (i.e., from the first year of the Depression to the last year the independent specialty luxury manufacturers offered meaningful competition) reveal the Darwinian effects of the Depression and the consolidation trends of the luxury automobile market. In addition, the regional appeal of some marques can be seen quite vividly—Auburn's 1934 cars thrived in the Midwest but failed in California and New York.

Some of the most interesting prestige models in the 1930s were built by manufacturers whose primary market thrust was less expensive motor cars: Marmon, Peerless (both originally luxury automobiles who later changed direction), Auburn, Buick, Nash, Reo, Graham, Hudson, Chrysler, Elcar, Jordan, Kissel, Roamer, Studebaker, and Willys-Knight (all moderate-price marques who went upmarket). Published state-by-state registrations did not segregate their models by price, so the exact impact of each is blurred by overall numbers. As such, only some of these cars are included in the following sales table. At the other end of the price spectrum were the cottage-industry size producers of exclusive automobiles: Duesenberg, duPont, Cunningham, Brewster, Ruxton, Doble, and Rolls-Royce—which do not have state-by-state (or in many cases overall) registrations. By the end of the 1930s, all specialty upmarket manufacturers had disappeared; 1936 data is reduced to nine marques.

Year-to-year comparisons of individual state registrations indicate some heroic measures taken to sell automobiles. Marmon's Missouri distributor raised sales to 400 cars in 1931, while that marque's nationwide sales fell some 60%. Franklin's Michigan 90% sales drop in 1931 is explained by a distributor problem surprisingly unresolved before the banks took over the company. Franklin's Michigan registrations for 1930 were up 10% or so from 1929's 120 cars, at a time when Franklin was losing sales overall, making the 1931 loss even more significant. The District of Columbia held good results for many marques: Cadillac's 1931 sales were only one car less than in 1930; Lincoln's 1932 sales bested both 1931 and 1930. Reo sales remained remarkably stable from 1932 to 1936.

The reason for Pierce-Arrow's sales increase in Michigan from 1931 to 1932 can be traced. Its long-time Detroit distributor, Wm. F. V. Neumann & Sons, was located at 6022–6040 Woodward Avenue, on the main northwest route out of Detroit (just past the General Motors Building or equidistant between downtown and the northwest suburbs). Two factory branches replaced Neumann in 1932, one also on Woodward but closer to downtown and a second (which still stands) at 3162 East Jefferson, between Detroit's center and its Grosse Pointe suburbs. Roy Faulkner, Auburn's crack salesman, joined Pierce-Arrow at the end of 1931 as head of its sales organization. He must have put a great deal into this situation. All other high-price competitors except Lincoln (which increased sales slightly) lost consider-

SELECTED STATE SALES REGISTRATIONS • 1930–1936

	YEAR	DC and 48 STATE TOTAL	AZ	CA	CO	CT	FL	GA	IL	IN	ME	MD	MA	MI	MN
AUBURN	1930	11270	9	897	72	289	87	45	1003	373	29	85	498	234	95
	1931	29535	39	3325	255	634	274	111	2374	1006	127	344	1523	1053	404
	1932	11645	9	1206	142	200	122	44	1038	384	30	239	469	508	133
	1933	5038	3	760	66	80	48	62	404	261	1	169	116	123	45
	1934	5536	0	614	63	63	193	76	600	401	2	160	86	155	67
	1935	5163	5	466	72	176	135	73	594	480	10	48	122	111	84
	1936	1848	7	144	36	63	33	22	266	215	2	10	51	46	28
CADILLAC	1930	12078	16	1472	54	402	121	72	869	187	91	112	694	862	104
	1931	11136	17	1156	55	359	71	76	955	159	71	93	586	667	115
	1932	6268	9	574	34	150	44	56	545	78	35	61	244	405	62
	1933	3903	5	373	23	86	23	23	347	44	17	34	174	192	49
	1934	6692	10	513	38	172	57	51	400	63	34	44	254	330	44
	1935	4899	15	865	42	186	89	71	576	103	43	91	309	389	59
	1936	11766	32	1357	74	330	189	136	1046	228	81	143	638	636	116
CHRYSLER	1930	60908	118	4599	503	1351	699	353	4001	1300	496	809	2627	1810	1459
	1931	52650	87	3443	390	1015	659	414	3205	1257	322	665	2175	2090	1267
	1932	26004	25	1972	255	451	289	260	1720	627	103	385	1036	1122	591
	1933	28677	29	1981	217	547	245	297	1901	616	93	518	1282	1125	516
	1934	28052	55	1624	338	447	359	347	1511	633	150	462	1035	1089	566
	1935	40536	104	3043	369	652	404	381	2923	1170	151	809	1489	1767	922
	1936	58698	223	5839	722	835	574	531	4329	1628	193	921	1749	2677	1316
CORD	1930	1879	3	258	12	26	39	12	287	93	4	9	72	60	16
	1931	1416	1	84	16	18	22	13	218	82	2	17	41	52	17
	1932	335	0	25	3	1	4	1	28	21	1	3	5	6	2
						NOT SOLD IN 1933, 1934, OR 1935									
	1936	1174	8	159	7	32	33	9	142	107	4	16	25	57	16
FRANKLIN	1930	7482	12	651	36	247	94	73	670	81	54	103	519	134	20
	1931	3881	3	249	14	116	61	35	244	60	36	67	328	13	17
	1932	1829	1	73	9	60	48	30	126	39	17	32	129	12	8
	1933	1329	0	79	4	45	23	18	117	4	11	11	114	7	10
	1934	360	0	17	3	16	11	4	26	1	0	15	21	3	2
LASALLE	1930	11262	22	1109	88	406	113	86	1089	148	86	137	819	583	173
	1931	6883	7	537	39	200	41	51	743	91	59	68	595	284	79
	1932	3846	3	370	22	108	29	24	389	43	34	41	271	208	53
	1933	3709	0	337	27	104	32	29	321	38	27	39	266	185	53
	1934	5182	15	522	60	93	77	98	345	112	42	56	277	405	51
	1935	11775	36	1402	80	260	194	154	845	244	52	126	573	921	131
	1936	13992	33	1676	89	286	254	191	1109	294	90	169	773	931	153

SOURCE: *Automotive Daily News* and R. L. Polk & Co.

MO	NH	NJ	NM	NY	NC	OH	OK	OR	PA	RI	TN	TX	VA	WA	WI	DC
230	65	843	15	2677	25	836	63	43	954	99	51	128	72	177	165	104
756	88	1821	4	5704	191	2190	113	129	2747	304	174	209	213	228	736	322
472	38	532	5	2160	115	853	107	38	1029	79	82	247	105	89	257	296
105	7	257	2	839	42	435	104	18	394	23	26	174	25	11	38	47
131	29	164	11	478	59	588	295	15	388	20	18	194	60	62	51	61
103	25	238	10	592	39	313	55	49	333	9	34	216	68	85	59	142
55	8	90	0	208	8	99	39	15	116	6	6	45	19	39	17	19
231	46	824	11	2550	70	673	133	36	932	92	82	275	63	80	200	106
192	36	866	15	2650	54	532	98	47	988	103	44	215	74	75	174	105
128	11	439	9	1629	28	348	64	19	493	47	33	123	59	36	139	76
72	10	243	3	1003	24	276	44	13	361	20	23	78	18	25	64	38
119	13	279	3	1040	33	262	54	27	381	43	30	137	26	40	68	66
127	23	408	5	1300	34	365	60	37	549	42	47	203	45	56	99	109
221	48	695	14	2118	87	689	136	80	854	118	91	413	73	109	167	162
1247	296	3183	132	8578	844	3188	762	420	7083	606	614	1999	896	1032	1449	347
1064	207	2989	91	9077	792	3043	436	398	5885	593	333	1635	789	652	1141	455
666	107	1393	35	4371	347	1443	273	174	3293	283	219	878	301	350	478	245
712	113	1370	63	4701	456	1999	322	227	3499	286	249	1083	312	358	489	317
597	81	992	105	3701	610	2006	432	281	3446	226	275	1521	330	407	547	331
901	123	1433	116	4695	704	2779	572	461	4627	322	391	1927	470	594	902	477
1126	172	2393	208	6248	754	4355	724	729	6876	434	575	2216	657	901	1156	710
39	3	71	1	350	4	105	20	6	115	14	15	29	15	22	37	10
51	0	63	0	273	7	106	11	11	89	6	3	29	11	18	38	11
10	0	22	0	121	0	20	0	0	18	0	0	4	7	6	2	3
							NOT SOLD IN 1933, 1934, OR 1935									
12	3	44	0	143	5	57	28	6	70	13	5	43	4	17	13	3
149	45	406	2	1523	46	607	92	86	750	66	55	184	57	114	121	50
75	44	249	3	849	16	279	30	43	611	55	22	64	7	43	41	34
31	18	99	1	460	2	130	11	11	233	39	13	39	12	36	8	18
34	6	69	0	377	3	70	5	17	133	24	5	25	6	21	6	18
10	3	23	0	107	1	19	1	6	28	7	6	3	0	10	2	1
279	28	737	22	1868	62	513	128	48	1037	112	108	268	99	75	169	91
146	30	499	6	1373	38	310	37	27	729	94	36	134	40	32	116	69
97	10	242	3	702	27	203	27	10	445	51	31	86	29	24	74	22
100	7	245	2	789	16	258	40	10	374	41	19	57	16	17	77	25
129	11	221	6	809	59	329	74	38	383	37	45	198	40	56	105	70
293	41	638	17	1724	103	685	157	89	943	68	118	408	103	125	206	165
305	33	721	18	2028	122	838	171	170	1105	112	148	497	104	134	205	202

SELECTED STATE SALES REGISTRATIONS • 1930–1936

	YEAR	DC and 48 STATE TOTAL	AZ	CA	CO	CT	FL	GA	IL	IN	ME	MD	MA	MI	MN
LINCOLN	1930	4356	9	435	21	74	50	36	516	79	21	39	214	188	56
	1931	3466	5	363	15	56	33	30	357	57	11	33	194	199	45
	1932	3175	5	358	16	44	27	23	259	59	11	15	184	228	58
	1933	3422	0	207	17	53	15	7	208	28	9	11	113	120	35
	1934	2370	4	173	13	34	28	22	192	38	7	11	112	139	31
	1935	2061	4	240	16	43	44	20	197	40	8	16	105	229	26
	1936	15567	70	1684	164	207	387	210	1107	355	62	146	521	1358	265
MARMON	1930	12369	52	699	185	253	151	72	854	754	80	91	608	514	171
	1931	5687	5	203	69	102	93	44	384	374	38	35	210	238	48
	1932	1365	0	50	9	21	87	24	77	121	5	3	47	65	5
	1933	86						NOT AVAILABLE							
PACKARD	1930	28318	68	2530	159	873	238	133	2440	413	191	363	1952	1241	549
	1931	16256	33	1267	78	502	128	86	1491	219	120	245	1001	664	341
	1932	11052	22	762	60	314	83	100	918	154	89	189	704	485	211
	1933	9081	14	696	64	273	49	88	845	116	52	146	626	443	184
	1934	6552	12	503	47	232	68	99	639	78	29	86	383	263	99
	1935	37653	108	3011	270	1052	425	493	2731	686	201	562	2125	2041	643
	1936	68772	234	8467	599	1288	877	871	5339	1628	386	995	3773	3895	1203
PEERLESS	1930	4021	18	222	12	63	3	0	382	63	37	68	291	74	26
	1931	1249	0	60	8	3	0	0	205	9	2	75	89	28	5
PIERCE-ARROW	1930	6795	8	583	54	219	46	34	407	70	31	93	594	111	93
	1931	4522	3	399	42	147	32	48	311	46	10	60	419	64	60
	1932	2692	0	240	24	51	16	21	239	30	11	39	202	94	22
	1933	2152	0	152	26	54	7	6	185	18	8	38	155	29	19
	1934	1740	0	147	17	58	13	8	191	17	7	33	127	23	22
	1935	875	0	91	12	26	3	5	49	16	6	29	74	10	15
	1936	787	0	88	22	23	15	0	46	5	2	22	79	12	6
REO	1930	11449	6	989	69	419	139	44	645	179	86	146	753	886	198
	1931	6791	6	541	55	182	82	48	414	126	68	104	412	470	161
	1932	3868	2	273	26	109	40	28	230	54	36	55	247	336	81
	1933	3623	0	299	35	124	40	30	185	45	42	37	272	293	79
	1934	3854	3	289	35	124	52	33	216	53	34	15	295	328	109
	1935	3894	0	340	43	97	52	18	222	70	12	12	226	528	110
	1936	3146	4	275	36	69	43	16	244	81	3	13	150	447	104
STUTZ	1930	814	5	57	19	27	1	2	156	29	3	6	42	4	5
	1931	384	1	25	9	4	1	1	76	24	8	3	4	0	3
							NO DATA FOR 1932, 1933, OR 1934								

MO	NH	NJ	NM	NY	NC	OH	OK	OR	PA	RI	TN	TX	VA	WA	WI	DC
102	13	174	4	977	37	232	49	30	296	34	42	121	35	29	49	47
88	19	167	4	834	16	166	23	20	278	32	24	60	21	18	44	44
97	16	150	1	720	18	165	24	26	233	23	16	64	23	30	30	58
65	6	101	5	474	26	95	17	20	177	19	16	47	13	23	29	24
60	14	93	4	454	19	106	29	15	162	15	30	50	18	18	18	25
56	5	104	1	447	21	131	33	15	193	27	21	72	20	16	28	27
296	60	604	66	1730	170	801	260	272	1024	86	140	664	173	271	303	158
355	69	580	19	1831	65	1005	91	99	1215	29	77	400	152	108	231	74
400	23	411	8	720	21	529	16	32	736	10	15	122	82	22	107	68
86	5	79	2	354	2	63	4	2	139	3	2	8	11	2	7	5
								NOT AVAILABLE								
570	90	2002	24	5360	131	1631	314	131	2975	218	223	525	235	238	421	356
319	80	1218	7	3320	75	840	129	63	1719	107	92	287	195	116	274	295
226	39	795	10	2429	55	592	103	40	1095	72	68	159	116	94	193	231
209	29	548	11	1901	51	555	41	41	979	46	51	128	93	39	139	142
151	23	421	5	1412	33	304	65	34	699	45	49	130	61	41	98	81
727	150	1926	55	6108	439	2043	367	266	4005	223	411	1187	487	353	929	570
1489	249	3732	143	9542	743	4360	535	566	6090	527	622	2187	858	823	1635	628
35	14	304	0	523	4	687	8	1	473	69	4	50	58	31	78	199
24	1	80	0	142	0	220	0	0	115	32	1	6	7	5	17	84
257	26	583	3	1443	17	309	112	28	706	109	93	226	59	32	140	67
176	16	433	4	916	18	205	50	32	382	92	28	157	48	34	81	61
123	3	298	1	624	10	85	25	8	194	47	13	73	23	10	48	30
116	8	208	1	531	5	125	24	10	163	45	5	46	13	14	24	31
54	7	123	0	363	5	106	13	9	147	42	4	64	10	17	24	25
27	2	42	0	109	1	37	10	5	130	15	4	49	23	8	14	25
28	1	50	0	102	0	32	17	4	101	8	1	34	10	9	7	19
229	127	494	8	1447	25	702	140	134	964	264	70	581	113	193	229	63
156	30	350	8	1122	17	387	39	71	440	155	35	255	51	119	149	27
143	22	193	2	736	6	220	28	28	367	47	16	104	22	53	67	14
91	34	151	7	658	26	204	18	40	364	71	14	27	15	38	93	4
82	41	153	6	614	11	249	34	49	387	82	7	78	36	48	72	16
68	36	156	7	427	18	262	16	62	362	40	8	116	36	45	137	9
73	21	63	5	201	9	221	109	75	233	12	14	86	20	35	109	6
39	1	39	1	162	0	58	6	1	30	1	8	8	8	1	14	3
17	1	23	1	96	0	30	1	0	9	2	4	5	3	6	2	1
							NO DATA FOR 1932, 1933, OR 1934									

able ground, making Pierce's doubling Detroit sales (statewide registrations increased 50%) quite a feat. As Detroit branch losses were hidden on Pierce-Arrow's financial statements (board of directors' reports indicate they were not disclosed there), the exact cost of this effort will never be known. But with its half dozen non-New York factory branches losing $364,914 for all 1932, the selling cost of each Detroit sale could have approximated the list price of many models.

Encouraged despite such economics, in 1933 Pierce-Arrow attempted to duplicate these sales results in the Bay Area of northern California. A long-time Studebaker dealer, Chester N. Weaver at Bush and Van Ness in San Francisco (one of the many "automobile row" buildings of the 1920s and 1930s still standing on Van Ness Avenue) and 2860 Broadway in Oakland, also representing Pierce-Arrow, transferred his business late in 1932. Jeff R. Townsend took over both showrooms and added a third, at 2600 Shattuck Avenue in Berkeley. A nifty logo, designed for the new distributor, was shown prominently in display ads next to Earle C. Anthony's Packards and Don Lee's Cadillacs that appeared regularly in the automobile section of Sunday's *San Francisco Chronicle*. Studebaker's bankruptcy kept Jeff Townsend's business from seeing the end of 1933.

OVERSEAS

A point nearly forgotten today is this period's worldwide demand for American automobiles. Unless restricted by quotas or high customs duties, they were the most popular selling cars in all price classes, everywhere. Luxury sales mirrored American results—Packard was the most popular high-price car, with an appeal similar to Mercedes-Benz in the 1990s. Dealers, whether housed in elaborate structures or modest garages, abounded. There were two Packard outlets in Paris, France: Barbezat, at 102 avenue des Champs-Elysées and 13 Quai de Boulogne, in the suburb of Boulogne-sur-Seine. An impressively housed outlet in Melbourne, Australia, sold in excess of 200 Packards per year before the Depression struck. E. L. Quarles had a Franklin showroom in Hamburg, Germany, and the Chrysler dealership in Hannover. Someone in Hungary managed to sell two Franklins in 1932—a time when each American luxury marque was lucky to sell even one car in that country. And there were intriguing one-of-a-kind situations: a lone Cunningham was licensed to roam the French Concession of Shanghai (but only that part of the city—separate licenses were required in the International Settlement and the Chinese Municipality). Philippines sales registrations for 1936 show a new Duesenberg coming into the country during the first half of the year.

The collapse of commodity prices in 1929 foretold the Depression's coming to the United States, and soon fostered the trade wars and exchange problems that extended the Depression worldwide. Some sales registrations from France; Cuba; the Philippines; eastern Canada (Ontario, Quebec, New Brunswick, Nova Scotia, and Prince Edward Island); Tokyo, Japan; and Rio de Janeiro, Brazil, reflect the changed demand for most of the American luxury marques.

France was considered a showcase for all automobile manufacturers. The annual automobile show, Le Salon de l'Automobile, in Paris in October, was a world-class event. For American manufacturers it was a market for dealers throughout Europe and North Africa, rather than a vehicle for retail sales to the French public. A separate coachbuilders' show, the Concours d'Elegance, was also held in Paris in June, showing off custom-made bodies on many American chassis. In April 1930 France increased its automobile tariffs. Anticipating problems, luxury dealers liquidated inventories in 1931, raising market share of some marques at the expense of their French counterparts. The following year the luxury market all but vanished.

Cuba had a relatively large number of luxury automobiles. It was a smart winter resort at the time, and was particularly vulnerable to the Depression. A total of 3,263 cars of all types were sold in the country in 1930, then 896 in 1931, a drop of nearly 75%. In November 1931 only three cars were imported into Cuba, one Auburn and two Chryslers.

OVERSEAS SALES REGISTRATIONS OF AMERICAN LUXURY AUTOMOBILES

	France		Cuba		Philippines		E.Canada		Tokyo	Rio de Janeiro
	1930	1931	1930	1931	1935	1936	1936	1937	1936	1930
Auburn	—	42	—	1	4	6	29	3	16	14
Cadillac	46	31	18	2	7	21	191	240	26	33
Chrysler	456	321	50	27	94	82	2291	3169	124	148
Cord	—	22	2	1	—	4	—	—	1	5
Duesenberg	—	—	—	—	—	1	—	—	—	—
Franklin	—	—	—	—	3	1	3	—	—	—
LaSalle	22	8	7	—	19	52	206	846	4	5
Lincoln	15	19	12	15	2	40	166	313	14	15
Marmon	42	21	52	—	—	—	—	—	—	6
Packard	133	76	34	6	40	64	1476	1888	60	55
Pierce-Arrow	4	6	16	—	3	6	22	5	2	9
Reo	—	—	12	3	4	3	191	11	—	3
Stutz	1	3	—	—	—	1	—	—	—	8

Source: Economic and Trade Notes *(various issues), United States Department of Commerce 1931–38.*

Studebaker and Pierce-Arrow shared this showroom near the Arc de Triomphe in Paris, France, at the beginning of 1930.

Despite the Depression, the Philippines represented a small but growing automobile market in the 1930s, helped by American military expenditures. Automobile sales registrations were considered news; *The Manila Times* published license plate numbers together with owners' names and addresses. Luxury car registrations were concentrated in both the capital of Manila and in Rizal province, to the east of the city. Sales registrations were distorted by the series of plantations that blanketed much of the country; many of the cars on those plantations never saw service outside of them.

Sales registrations for eastern Canada reflect complete domination by American manufacturers. Canada was naturally most marques' largest market outside the United States. Many assembled their cars there to avoid import duties. Leftover models of marques gone out of business often sold some time after production ended—as the three Franklins in 1936 data.

Japan's automobile market in the 1930s was the reverse of what it is today—modest in size (about the same number as were sold in the state of Tennessee), with most cars being American. Domestic Japanese automobile production was just beginning at the time. Sales registration data was kept on a city-by-city basis. Increasing military and political censorship in the country made Tokyo registrations for 1936 the last available during the 1930s.

Rio de Janeiro, Brazil, was one of the best overseas markets for American luxury automobiles in the late-1920s. The number and variety of both popular marques and obscure names are intriguing: Stearns-Knight and Locomobile continued to be seen in sales registration records into 1930. The collapse of coffee prices in mid-1929, together with a revolution in 1930, destroyed the automobile market quickly: total sales registrations for 1930 were less than 5% of 1929. The economic shock was felt first in Sao Paulo, the center of the coffee industry. Rio, then the country's capital, continued some semblance of normalcy into 1930. By the mid-1930s the Brazilian automobile market had improved, but it never regained sales equal to those in the late 1920s.

The Depression

One of the best chronicles of the sense of the 1930s' changing automotive scene is an unexpected source: *The New Yorker* magazine. Legendary editor Harold Ross may have been a car buff, for among the letters from Paris and London and innumerable book reviews was "Motors," a column complete with its own cartoon. During the new car season there were also "The Automobile Salon" and "The Automobile Show," reports of the weeks before and after the event.

In the 1920s this automotive writing was done by Nicholas Trott. He was not as witty as *Country Life*'s novelist-in-residence Eric Hatch, allowing Hatch's work to remain the definitive 1920s specialty automotive reporting. However, at the stroke of 1930, *The New Yorker* introduced a new automotive journalist, G. F. T. Ryall, with the pen name "Speed." He wrote for the 1930s only, succeeded in 1940 by Lincoln Barnett, who was identified by the initials L. K. B. (George Ryall was best known in another guise, Audax Minor, *The New Yorker*'s racetrack columnist for 52 years. When Ryall died in 1979, the magazine's anecdote-filled obituary did not mention his automotive writing.)

Speed cited wheelbase lengths, observed colors and design trends, and delighted in automotive rumors (he announced the Franklin V-12 one year early). In the annual reviews of the Automobile Show at Grand Central Palace. The 1933 show brought out Speed's incisiveness. It was the first year without the companion Automobile Salon. But Speed noticed the Salon's influence in the show's exhibits: particularly the variety of colors in the cars. Chrysler's exhibit was six models, all painted the same shade of gray, placed on a cream-colored carpeting, with salesmen wearing matching suits. While 1933 was the turning point in the acceptance of streamlining, and Speed discussed this, his most important observation that year was that smaller, less expensive cars were the equals in comfort and mechanical features of the best cars just a few years earlier.

Speed kept engineering discussions to a minimum but never failed to mention anomalies of important technical points. He dismissed the 1934 hullabaloo about General Motors's "knee action" ride because it was the same system of thick springs used on 1920 Lancia automobiles. Speed dutifully covered Chrysler's relentless engineering progress in the 1930s, noting that the hoods of the new Airflow models worked just like those found on World War I-era electric cars.

When coachbuilt motor cars began losing favor with the public, Speed also took that point of view. He became excited about Hudsons, particularly their interior trimming. In his report on the November 1937 Automobile Show, the new Graham "shark-nose" models received more praise than the Cadillac Sixty Special sedan, also new that year.

In his column, accessories were always given good coverage. The premier New York accessory shop in the 1930s was Nil Melior (who moved from different locations in Manhattan's West 50s to the new Waldorf-Astoria Hotel). He supplied the striking radiator screens at the 1931 Salon (a luxury fad until New York City taxicab fleets imitated it), and the Lalique crystal radiator mascots and MoToVoX brand musical horns. Melior was also the importer of the big Marchal headlights seen on super deluxe cars such as the last Duesenberg, Rudolph Bauer's Rollson-bodied transformable town car.

CHRONOLOGY

In the 1930s, at almost precisely three-year intervals, significant automotive milestones took place. Beginning in 1931, the Depression took hold, fatally wounding all independent specialty luxury car manufacturers (and most of the coachbuilding industry along with them). In 1934 streamlined design and engineering advances—not coachbuilt models—were the emphasis of the prestige marques. Although 1937 was the best automotive year of the mid- and late-1930s, it was the last year in which the independent luxury cars had any measurable participation—after that, the names just dropped off the list. As 1940 began, Cadillac, Packard, and Lincoln each decided against going forward with their prestigious multicylinder car lines. Chrysler had since put aside making the Imperial a trend-setter and relegated its best models—which were very special—to show car status.

The first two years of the Depression were similar to the recessions we experience today. Automobile sales behaved accordingly. Early in the spring of 1931 there were definite economic indicators that business was on the mend. Suddenly, in May, the largest bank in Austria failed, aggravating numerous European business problems. As the summer ended, there was a sharp tightening of interest rates in the United States to protect currency exchange rates. Business sentiment turned pessimistic. Then came retaliatory trade measures resulting from Hawley-Smoot tariffs and quotas. The crop failures in the Southwest (that led to the Dust Bowl), the bank closings and business failures, all worsened. For the next 18 months, the economy steadily declined. By one account the automobile industry was operating at 20% of capacity in 1932. This caused a precipitous drop in Detroit real estate values, which in turn placed pressure on the Michigan banking system, and on one Detroit bank in particular, early in 1933.

Old business differences surfaced when United States Senator James Couzens, a former associate of Henry Ford, challenged an application for federal government assistance by the Union Guardian Trust Company, part of a banking group in which Ford was an investor and Edsel Ford a director. The bank needed to raise cash to pay growing deposit withdrawals. The governor of Michigan publicly took sides against the Fords, then retracted his remarks (Henry Ford offered to freeze his own deposits in the bank for capital). All this increased the run on the bank and threatened larger banks in the Guardian group. To stop it, the governor called a one-week bank holiday. Because of the governor's personal problems—only six weeks in office and he was reportedly fighting garnishee proceedings against his salary—there appeared to be widespread acceptance of his actions.

When Franklin Roosevelt was inaugurated as President two weeks later, he followed Michigan's lead and closed all the banks in the country. This grueling catharsis—which led to Studebaker's bankruptcy (which in turn stopped its financial coddling of Pierce-Arrow) and aggravated Reo's finances since 70% of its bank deposits were tied up in the Michigan crisis—revived faith in the banking system. Combined with New Deal spirit (and the economic boost from the end of Prohibition), the Depression began to abate. Overall automobile registrations for 1933, up 42%, reflected it; the numbers for luxury car makers, down 27%, did not. In hindsight, this data's message was quite clear: the market for big glamorous automobiles would soon be over. But at the time it was realistic to expect that prosperity's return would renew demand for the luxury car. Everyone that could geared up for just that, but hedged their bets by planning or introducing less expensive models, as well.

1934

At the end of 1933 the National Recovery Act, a part of the New Deal popularly known as the NRA, was passed. It was meant to stimulate business but actually dealt the independent automobile manufacturer a setback with regulations proscribed in the Motor Vehicle Retailing Trade Code. Some requirements were minor: establishments had to be kept open a minimum of 52 hours per week; minimum pay for labor was 40 cents per hour. Other mandated practices went to the core of a dealer's negotiating position in the sale of a car: automobiles sold as demonstrators had to be registered with a local trade association and were not to be sold for less than full price until used for at least 60 days and operated for 3,500 miles. More damaging was the fixing of used car allowances. Independents typically gave the buyer an incentive in an extra trade allowance when a car was sold; now that advantage was more difficult to achieve (unless the factory raised its discount to the selling agency).

During the Depression used car depreciation rates were significantly different from those of today. It would be correct to say the value of a luxury automobile did not depreciate, it disappeared. There are some vivid examples. A 1930 Cord phaeton-sedan with a list price of $3,295 had an appraised value of $975, or 30% of list, at the end of the following model year. A 1930 Cadillac V-16 sedan valued at $2,500 retained 40% of its original $6,225 list price, a better ratio. The numbers for discontinued marques were overwhelming: "The Automobile Exchange" section of the September 7, 1934, *New York Times* contained an ad for a 1933 Franklin V-12 limousine, originally $5,400, for $1,250. An April 1937 listing of cars for sale by the Lincoln dealer in New York City, Ford Motor Sales Company, priced a one-year-old Zephyr sedan (model not given) at $895, about half its list. This suggests the new medium-price luxury cars were more economic to own on a depreciation basis alone.

The many technical and styling changes in the 1934 automobiles were of watershed quality. Chrysler had begun popular advocacy of high compression engines and four wheel hydraulic brakes back in the mid-1920s. Another leap forward came in 1930–1931 with the synchromesh transmission. For 1934 the emphasis was on ride. There were two simultaneous approaches to this. General Motors's introduction of independent front suspension—often referred to as "knee action"—contrasted with Chrysler's radical Airflow engineering, which improved ride by structural and design changes throughout the vehicle. Concurrently, rounded streamline styling took hold. The differences between Chrysler and non-Chrysler approaches (one opinion compared "the Airflow and obsolete models") were enormous.

The Airflow's external design was so unusual as to limit demand for the car. This unfortunately detracted from its incredibly advanced engineering details. The motor was pushed forward, to be on top of rather than behind the front axle (Franklin enthusiasts will recall that marque used a mild variation of this concept, with the false radiator ahead rather than parallel to the front axle). Having the car's weight distributed towards its extremities reduced pitching. Placing the steering mechanism ahead of the front axle allowed for softer springing. The result was a ride of "phenomenal smoothness." The all-steel body, built as a bridge truss frame, contributed to the smooth ride. But because this construction discouraged coachbuilder modifications, there would be no custom-bodied versions.

In sharp contrast, Cadillac's knee action altered the front axle to improve ride, a change tucked away where it could not be seen. The improvement was not as significant as Chrysler's but was there, nonetheless. Cadillac's exterior styling incorporated evolutionary streamlining that set an industry standard: details such as the narrow vertical radiator grille were seen on a number of other marques (in all price ranges) the following year.

The Airflow concept, with whatever mistakes were made in its execution, introduced the next type of luxury car; a progression that had come from individual custom to series custom was continued in the charismatic production model. There were no coachbuilder bodies (but former coachbuilders helped design and build the prototypes) or elaborate options for interior trimming, but the unusually stylish bodies were well engineered and more practical. The show cars of the 1933 World's Fair, such as Pierce's Silver Arrow, suggested this direction, but it was the Airflow that put it into production. The Cord 810 of 1936 and Cadillac's Series Sixty Special of 1938 were other top-of-the-line versions. The Lincoln Zephyr also had this quality on a more modest scale, while the Continental series modified from it perfected the type.

By the end of 1936 the American economy appeared normal. The Depression seemed tamed. Overall automobile production numbers were very good but the competitive pressures on the small independent manufacturers remained as intense as ever. Earlier in the year Brewster, Cunningham, and Reo had given up; later, Auburn announced deferral of its 1937 models. The Depression and streamlining had changed motor fashion away from individuality and the coachbuilt ideal. The modest new luxury cars—Lincoln Zephyr, Packard 120, LaSalle, and Cord 810—were the center of attention. The registration numbers confirm the swiftness of the transition.

THE 1937 AUTOMOBILE SHOW

The first of the 1937 automobile shows took place in early November 1936 in New York City at the Grand Central Palace exhibition hall (still standing one block east of Grand Central Station). Of the great non-Detroit specialty manufacturers only Auburn's Auburn-Cord-Duesenberg trio and Pierce-Arrow remained. No one would think anything was out of place seeing the *Automotive Daily News* headline for the show. "Ford, Willys and Pierce Ready For New York Show" appeared in inch-high block letters. Front page photos and copy were evenly divided among the three manufacturers. For Pierce-Arrow this was a public relations dream come true: it sold only 22 cars in October 1936, yet shared the limelight on the front page with a company selling almost a million automobiles a year. (Perhaps that helped Pierce sales jump to 90 cars in November.)

This was the second year in a row for a November show. The industry moved the introduction of its new models forward, from January to November (when the defunct Automobile Salon once began) to mitigate seasonality of sales. President Roosevelt was delighted at this change and wrote to Alvan MacCauley, head of Packard and the Automobile Manufacturers Association, in a letter published on the front page of the *Automotive Daily News*.

Despite the fact that 1937 was a good automobile sales year, the promised 1937 Auburn never materialized. That summer the first signs of the coming 1938 recession began. In August, E. L. Cord sold his interest in Auburn. By September, the showrooms were closing down. A determined group of Buffalo, New York, businessmen kept Pierce-Arrow alive into 1938, making a handful of models. But the recession prevented the company from raising capital. A Cincinnati, Ohio, parts supplier forced sale of the company by the bankruptcy court in May 1938. At the same time a receiver in Indianapolis, Indiana, was setting the date for sale of assets for what remained of Stutz.

1940

At the end of the 1930s there was a World's Fair in New York City. Coincidental with the second end of the Depression (the 1938 recession proved it was not quite over), it had a landmark quality in its exhibits and in the impact of its theme, "The World of Tomorrow." Each pavilion, every boulevard and side street in the Fair shared this focus. From an automotive point of view, this was all well and good, but the automobile exhibits were limited to the Big Three manufacturers, General Motors, Chrysler, and Ford. No single model stood out, such as the Silver Arrow of the 1933 Chicago World's Fair (but then there was no longer a Pierce-Arrow to make one). While the casual observer was taken by this spectacle, he may have realized that "The World of Tomorrow" included only the Big Three. The Trylon and Perisphere, symbols of the Chicago World Fair, pointed toward a chillingly accurate prediction for the U.S. automobile industry.

The 1940 automobile shows left no doubt that the time of special automobiles was quickly passing. In *The New Yorker*, Speed cautioned, "don't expect to be overwhelmed by the originality of the new body designs." *Business Week* had an equally negative assessment. "More similarity of Design" was the subhead of its write-up of the show, which noted that new automobile designs were either quickly imitated or abandoned. The trend began in the mid-1930s, when Cadillac/LaSalle introduced the tall, narrow-radiator grille. Then in 1938, the redesigned front end of the Lincoln Zephyr put a wide grille in the lower front end of the car, a look called "low cooling." By 1940, nearly everyone had taken up the Lincoln concept.

Chrysler's engineering prowess took center stage at these last prewar automobile shows. It expanded its work on ride and adapted an English flywheel transmission used on Daimlers and Lanchesters, first to its Imperial line in 1939, then on all Chrysler makes for 1940. Chryslers were completely redone for 1940, inside and out. Redesign was no accident; changing wheelbase lengths required new bodies. The new body had much simpler lines, following the Lincoln Zephyr's lead.

Coachbuilt automobiles garnered little attention. Packard's discontinuing its twelve cylinder cars merited less than a full sentence in *Business Week*'s review of the 1940 New York Automobile Show. Speed took more notice. He openly criticized the dated look of many models Packard was selling in 1940 but reserved kudos for the show-stopping quality of Packard's Darrin-bodied Super Eight convertible victoria.

Not much could be said about Cadillac. Its eye-catching Series Sixty Special sedan was now four years old and was most noticed for passing on a resemblance throughout the Cadillac line. The new Lincoln Continental, on the other hand, caught the reviewers off guard. Henry Ford did not exhibit his cars with the others at Grand Central Palace, but rather at a special showing at Ford's factory branch on Broadway and 54th Street. This alone would have dampened coverage of the new models a bit but the Lincoln Zephyr convertible victoria that we now call the Continental felt the full thrust of this separation from the show. It was noticed and admired by the press, but not with the awestruck remarks the car always commands today.

If any elaborate custom-bodied cars appeared in the show they were not mentioned. A neat Chrysler town car by Derham escaped display, as did the breathtaking Rollson-bodied Packards, some with sunroofed sedan bodies. Californians Bohman and Schwartz may not even have been mentioned.

At the height of the Depression, automobile manufacturers had almost stopped this annual display because people had only looked. Now everyone was buying and the shows were economic. But the interest lay in push-button windows, automatic transmissions, and motorized convertible tops. When Packard offered air conditioning as a 1941 option, no one bothered to describe the sort of body it was in. Whatever it was seemed less important.

In 1934 a Pierce-Arrow magazine ad had lured the reader showing a sedan partially hidden by darkness and accompanied with the statement, "if this be magic make the most of it." By 1940 it was not clear whether the magic was gone or too few people wanted the challenge.

This Willoughby-bodied Pierce-Arrow all-weather town car was built for the 1929, 1930, and 1931 model years. It had a detachable cast aluminum roof for the driver, which gave the car the look of a limousine when in place. The rambling body molding was a Willoughby trademark. This 1930 model had a list price of $6,825.

Portfolio
1930 – 1942

A boldly painted roadster (the light color trim in front extends over the entire rear deck) was one of three Franklin models exhibited at the 1930 Paris automobile show, Le Salon de l'Automobile. A Dietrich-designed Deauville close-coupled sedan is behind the folded top of the roadster.

(opposite) Franklin received a face-lift for the 1930 model year. Coachbuilder Ray Dietrich subtly revised the deCausse design, most notably changing the false radiator motif.

When Cunningham modernized the look of its cars in the late-1920s, it gave up a distinctive exterior design, and chose to mimic Cadillac. Enthusiasts will point out drum headlights and a pronounced cowl as distinguishing marks, but this 1930 V-9 touring car (the V-9 being the model designation; the engine was a V-8) could pass for a Cadillac to others.

Cords neatly fit into boxcars for their journey to the salesroom.

A Marmon "Big Eight" sedan at the Oakland, California, airport on February 28, 1930. This model had a 136-inch wheelbase chassis with a 125 HP straight eight engine.

The new front-wheel drive Ruxton may have been the most attractive automobile of 1930. This roadster, a phaeton, a sedan, and a town car were its four standard body styles—all on a 130-inch wheelbase chassis with a 269 cubic inch Continental straight eight engine rated at 100 HP. Prices began at $3,195. Production did not last one full year.

Cannon Ball Baker, the "automobile speed king," crossed the Miami, Florida, city line on the Tamiami Trail on March 4, 1930, at 8:15 A.M. in a record-breaking test of the new Franklin.

Baker (right) set what was said to be the world's intercity speed record that day, going between Ft. Myers and Miami, a distance of 133 miles, in one hour and 46 minutes. At times the car ran between 85 and 90 MPH. He left Ft. Myers at 6:30 A.M. in a seven passenger sedan with two passengers and 360 pounds of concrete added for traction. During the trip, 185 bridges were crossed, 51 automobiles passed. Speed had to be reduced to an average of 65 MPH negotiating the 49 turns on the road.

Parts of the Tamiami Trail still resemble what they were during Baker's journey, giving today's drivers an excellent appreciation of this accomplishment.

This 1931 Lincoln close-coupled sedan, made to look like a convertible sedan, is by an unknown coachbuilder. All the details in this design stand out—thick chrome window frames, a special front bumper, four exposed door hinges, a trunk incorporated into the body (unusual for 1931). The dark cloth spare tire cover, used when metal covers were the rage, deletes the visual impact of the spare. The roof's color is repeated in the thick band (sill edge) above the running board.

The dramatic styling suggests the work of Rollston or Walter Murphy. But the door handles, often a coachbuilder's distinguishing mark, appear to be Brewster's, who was also capable of bold design.

One of the first signs of changing automotive style was coachbuilder bodies on inexpensive chassis. Edsel Ford's interest in coachwork ensured Ford's participation in this.

Parisian carrossier Willy Van den Plas (not to be confused with the Belgian coachbuilder Van den Plas or its English licensee, Vanden Plas), built this convertible victoria body on a Ford Model A that was exhibited at the June 1931 International Custom Body Show in Paris. It had an ivory body with dark blue windshield pillar extending to the running board (one of this coachbuilder's trademarks), sky blue fenders, whitewall tires, and Frank et Cie. Chromos brand bumpers. Ford brought the car back to the United States and subdued the color mix by darkening the fender color and using blackwall tires.

Rollston, an extraordinary New York City coachbuilder known for its one-of-a-kind bodies, built this convertible sedan on a Packard chassis.

There is a fine balance in the car's traditional-style body molding: Rollston's trademark scroll-shaped door handles, a top that folds into a slender tailored rectangle, and chrome plated spare tire covers. The sun visor, a 1920s styling feature, gives the car a slightly European look.

Pasadena, California, photographer Dick Whittington shot this Cord L-29 convertible coupe as its tall owner was about to demonstrate the ease (or difficulty) of getting in and out of such a low car.

Russian emigré Count Alexis de Sakhnoffsky was in charge of design at the Hayes Body Co. of Grand Rapids, Michigan, during the 1930s. He stands between two of his best known designs of the period—the bantam-size American Austin and a one-off L-29 Cord coupe (built six inches lower than production Cords) that won the Grand Prix de Monaco design competition.

Sakhnoffsky's work was also seen on production Marmon (page ii and 45), Peerless, and Chrysler (page 132) models.

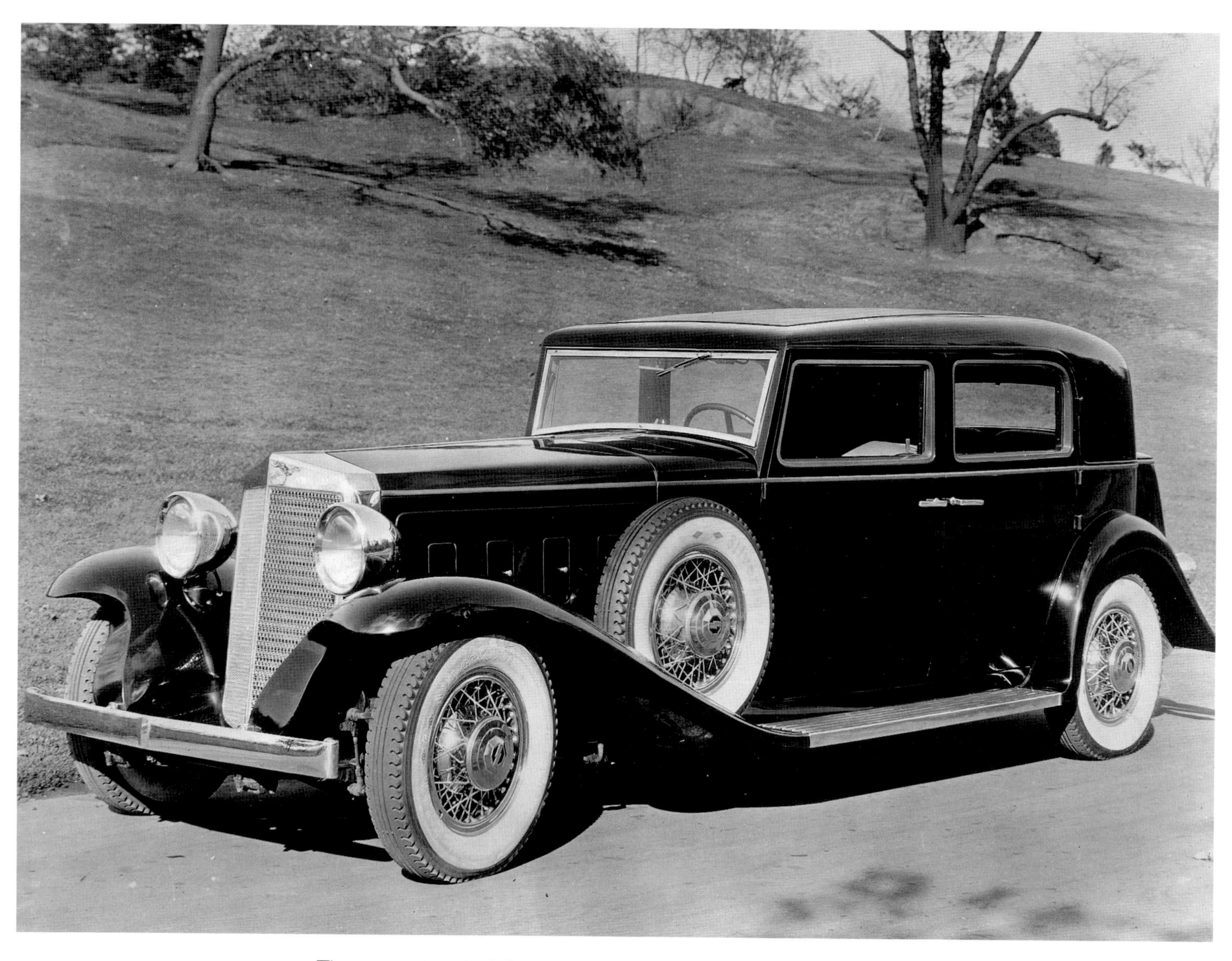

The crown jewel of the twenty-sixth annual Automobile Salon in New York in December 1930 was Marmon's new sixteen cylinder engine close-coupled sedan. It was extraordinary for both its engineering and its styling—no other production model tried to erase so many of the visual differences between the body and the chassis. Only 390 would be built.

Hebrank-Hunter Co., Ltd., Marmon's Oakland, California, dealer, located at 3435 Broadway, put on this impressive display of sixteen cylinder automobiles in their appropriately severe Art Deco showroom in August 1931.

The convertible coupe in the foreground, on a 145-inch wheelbase chassis with the engine rated at 200 HP, had a $5,370 list price.

Airports were popular settings for commercial photographs of all automobiles. These two 1931 Pierce-Arrow scenes were taken some 3,000 miles apart. The convertible coupe (above), in Oakland, California, stands in front of an Autogiro, a plane with a helicopter rotor that was a fad at the time. The limousine (opposite) is in Baltimore, Maryland.

This Waterhouse-bodied convertible victoria on Packard's 145-inch wheelbase chassis was shown at the November 1930 Automobile Salon in Chicago's Drake Hotel. The car was painted black with ivory striping and a light gray Burbank top. The interior was finished in Velveau tan leather patterned in diamond-shaped tufts (an unusual detail for a coachbuilder known for plain interiors). Reading lights were fitted into the left and right corners of the top's rear bow.

One interesting construction detail was windshield pillars of manganese bronze. Both pillars and cowl were covered with sheet aluminum to keep paint from breaking at the joints.

The convertible victoria was Waterhouse's most popular body style. Some 125 were built in its Webster, Massachusetts, shop from the late 1920s to 1932, when the firm closed down.

Chrysler's redesign of its 1931 models, coupled with the introduction of an eight cylinder engine to supplement its six cylinder cars, further improved the marque. These models were the stars of many 1931 automobile shows, including this one in France.

A 1931 Packard sport phaeton drives through the gate of the Greenbrier Hotel in White Sulphur Springs, West Virginia.

(opposite) Some of the Greenbrier's fleet of Buick sedans and limousines.

Martin Walter, Ltd., was a prolific English coachbuilder (using chassis as diverse as Austin and Daimler) in the port city of Folkestone. One observation of their work at the time, "typically striking coachwork," describes this Chrysler Imperial Eight sedan. While a significant departure from the flamboyance of the factory body style, it remains every bit as appropriate for the chassis.

Derham designed and built this series custom Franklin brougham for the 1929, 1930, and 1931 model years. This is the 1931 version.

The lack of sidemount spare tires on this 1931 Franklin victoria brougham makes it appear longer than its 125-inch wheelbase. With a list price of $2,345, it was one of the least expensive 1931 Franklin models.

A Cadillac V-12 sedan was photographed in an advertising display.

In the summer of 1932, Auburn's twelve cylinder model made record-breaking runs—averaging 89 MPH for the 500-mile run—at Muroc Dry Lake in California. The preparations for such an event seem incredibly simple by today's standards.

The site of Muroc Dry Lake is now known as Edwards Air Force Base.

Baltimore, Maryland's, Mt. Vernon Square has changed little since this Auburn sedan was photographed there in 1932 to promote Seiberling tires. A convertible sedan (opposite) is parked in a quieter setting. The original owners of the cars are written in the bottom of the photographs.

SEIBERLING AIR COOLED TIRES ON THE CAR OF
J. B. MANN. PRESIDENT ANNEX LAUNDRY
SEIBERLING DUO TREAD

This Stutz cabriolet coupe, about 1932, used a vertical windshield at a time when slanted windshields were the standard.

One of the last Stutz automobiles built was photographed on October 24, 1932. The body seems unusually tall for a Stutz and suggests the stateliness of cars in the early 1920s.

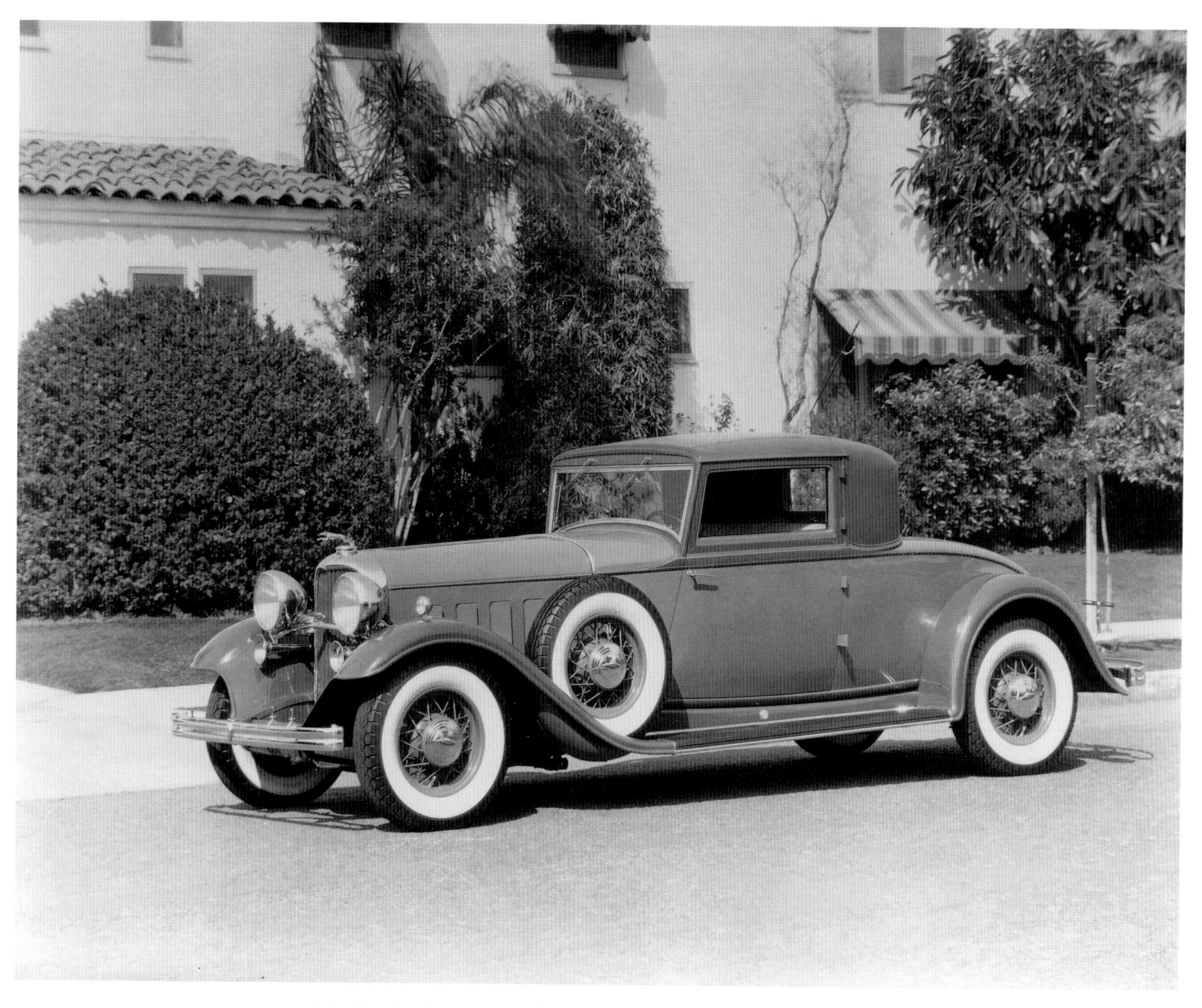

A Judkins-bodied coupe with a list price of $5,350 (above) and a Brunn all-weather brougham with a list price of $7,000 (opposite) were two of Lincoln's 1932 series custom body designs. Both were on the KB 145-inch wheelbase chassis with a 150 HP twelve cylinder engine.

Coachbuilders like to distinguish their work with specially designed hardware, unique to their firm. However, Lincoln standardized the door handles of its series customs.

The battle of the multicylinder engines for the 1932 model year started when Packard, Pierce-Arrow, Franklin, Lincoln, and Auburn all introduced twelve cylinder engines.

This is the debut of Packard's twelve cylinder car, called Twin Six, unveiled from a cover of heavy wrapping paper. The car, a model 906 sedan on a 147-inch wheelbase chassis with a 160 HP engine, was purchased by the president of the Libby-Owens-Ford Glass Company.

This 1932 Pierce-Arrow club brougham was a promotional giveaway by Pierce's Baltimore, Maryland, distributor, C. H. Reeves & Co.

C. Henry Reeves took over the Baltimore factory distributorship (named Foss-Hughes) in 1926. It was located at 1313–1315 Cathedral Street, across from the Mt. Royal railroad station. When Reeves switched to representing Lincoln in September 1933, Pierce-Arrow reestablished a facory branch three blocks south, on the corner of Eager, at number 1001. The Reeves building is gone, having made way for a parking garage several years ago. But 1001 Cathedral has been restored.

Walter Chrysler's son, Walter P. Chrysler, Jr., drove this handsome LeBaron-bodied roadster, one of three built on the 1932 Chrysler Imperial 135-inch wheelbase chassis. A patron of the arts, Chrysler later traded the car for a painting.

Two 1932 Reo Royale sedans, photographed near Lake Merritt in Oakland, California, show the effects of different trim and two-tone paint on identical body styles. The soft curves of Amos Northup's design accentuate one of the most handsome classic era automobiles.

The Duesenberg exhibit at the October 1932 Paris Salon consisted of a 1931 Franay-bodied town car (foreground), a chassis, and a Fernandez-bodied convertible coupe famous for being sold to actress Greta Garbo.

Duesenberg's Paris dealer, Motor Deluxe, located at 12 rue de Berri, had a knack for promotion—entering numerous races and coachwork competitions—that attracted royalty and heads of state as customers. There was a burst of sales activity in late 1931, with 14 cars selling in four months, a number approximating Duesenberg's entire 1932 American sales.

Duesenbergs often came back to the factory for modifications if they were to be resold. This undated photo of a Franay-bodied convertible sedan, said to be originally owned by Queen Marie of Yugoslavia, shows the substitution of racing type fenders and running boards to change the car's look.

Dr. Edward C. Worden, the chemist known for his cellulose research, stands with his spectacular Pierce Silver Arrow on the grounds of his Millburn, New Jersey, home in mid-1933. The thickness of the open door, nearly a foot wide at one point, suggests some of the features within. A spare tire is concealed between the front wheel and front door. The car was built at the Studebaker factory in South Bend, Indiana, using Pierce's 139-inch wheelbase chassis with a 175 HP twelve cylinder engine.

Worden loved to show off his Silver Arrow. He would drive the car on business to corporate headquarters to maximize its attention-getting qualities. It had one flaw, a problem with the automatic choke when the engine was warm. There could be trouble starting it, grinding down the battery in front of the admiring crowd the car always commanded.

A 1933 Auburn convertible coupe gleams in the Indiana sunshine (to the extent of producing white spots on the photograph from reflected light).

The whitewall tires and two-tone paint are primarily for publicity; the Depression discouraged most owners from ordering such attention-grabbing details.

President and Mrs. Roosevelt rode in a 1933 Pierce-Arrow touring car after inauguration ceremonies on March 4, 1933.

Two Pierce-Arrow touring cars flank the Roosevelts' car as the parade turns off Pennsylvania Avenue onto 15th Street. Pierce-Arrow had an agreement with the United States government, often referred to as the "Pierce-Arrow contract," which required the use of Pierce cars in highly visible situations in exchange for a nominal one-dollar-per-year charge. When presidents began using non-Pierce cars on official business, there was always a question raised about the contract. Warren Harding's Locomobile was the first case in point. Then Edsel Ford gave Calvin Coolidge a Lincoln. The results of Ford's efforts are behind Roosevelt's car—the light body colors and white-wall tires of the three Lincolns (a 1932 touring car between two 1933 models) must have been chosen to focus attention away from the dark Pierce-Arrows.

At the 1933 Chicago World's Fair Duesenberg exhibited a supercharged sedan with a Rollston body called the Arlington. It quickly became known as the "Twenty Grand" because of its price.

This is an exceptional design, one of the best of the classic era. The interior, done in what was called "plain style," is breathtaking. But in the context of the time, when other manufacturers were embracing streamlining in their designs, the Arlington was not a commercial success. No one bought it until it had been repainted and fitted with different wheels and fenders.

190

This seven-passenger sedan was one of Franklin's twelve cylinder models for 1933 and 1934. Designed by LeBaron, it is a different approach to streamlining than other luxury car manufacturers used. This model sits on a 144-inch wheelbase chassis, with a 150 HP V-12 engine. The price in 1934 was $2,995, a $1,000 reduction for the same model as 1933.

Business Week reported Edsel Ford bought one of the first Brewsters. Although the archival label in the photograph indicates it is a coachbuilt Ford, close examination suggests it is Ford's Brewster, fitted with a Ford radiator shell and a Lincoln greyhound radiator mascot.

Carl Beck, Brewster's designer, is said to have drawn the car's lines (with Brewster's impresario John Inskip probably helping, since he also drew).

The final inspection of this Lincoln convertible sedan took place on April 27, 1934, amidst the vastness of the shipping room.

37-L-1
38-L-1
58806
4/27/34

With appropriate fanfare, a 1934 Pierce-Arrow club sedan was awarded the Brussels Cup. Many European countries did not allow Pierce-Arrow's fender mounted headlights, forcing their replacement with a variety of bracket mounted styles. It made a significant change in the look of the car.

24532

The Chrysler Airflow was the most controversial automobile of 1934. Its technical advances—such as the all-steel unitized type body construction and the cab forward passenger compartment that widened the interior of the car by nearly a foot, were considered cancelled by the car's exterior design. But the angle at which southern California photographer Dick Whittington shot this 128-inch wheelbase coupe reveals allure in the contrasting body lines.

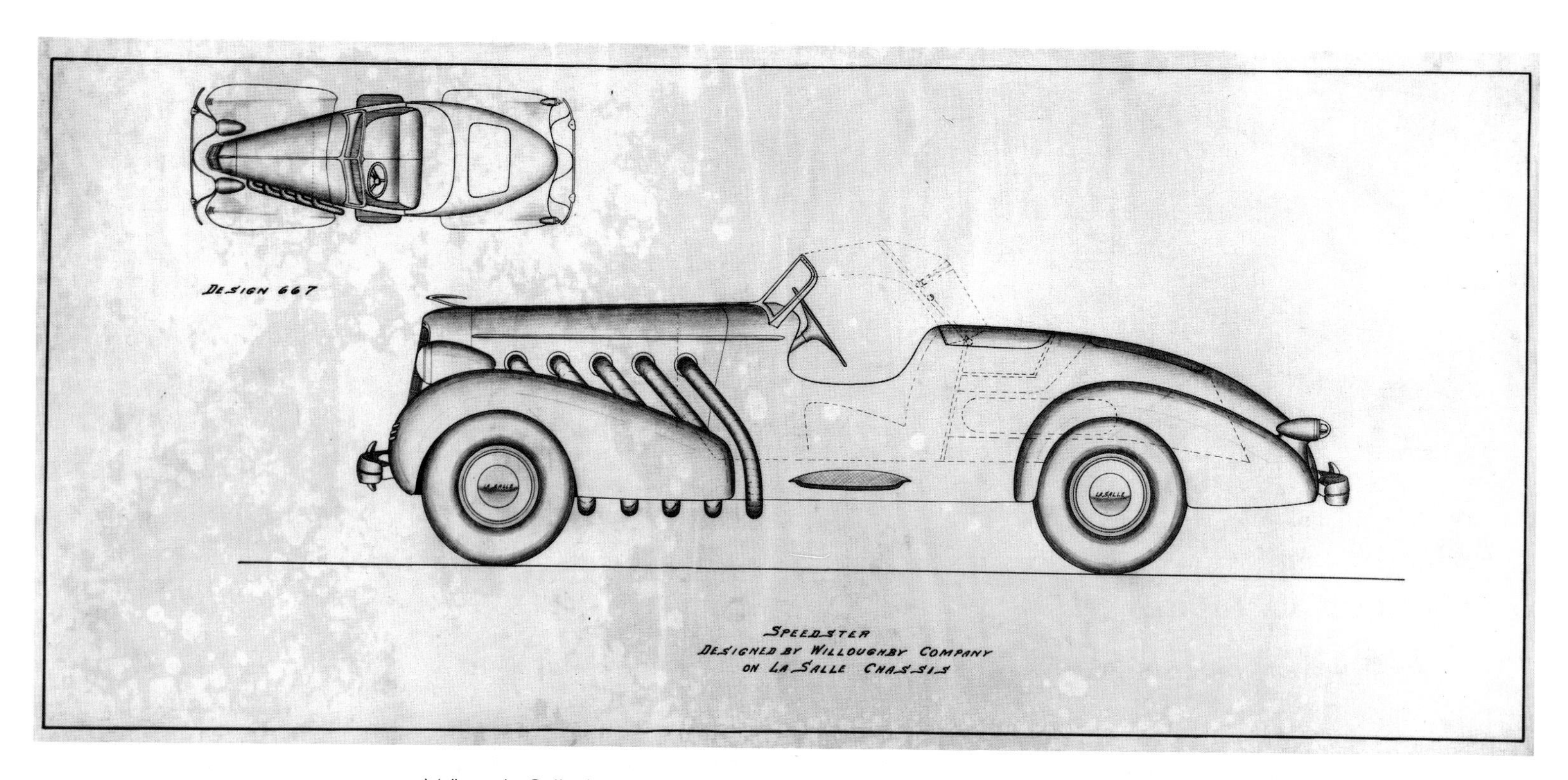

When LaSalle lowered prices in 1934 to expand market share, it also must have contemplated an Auburn-style image, as evidenced by this Willoughby supercharged speedster proposal. It is not known to have been built, leaving the photograph of Miss Florida, Elsie Weems (opposite), with her 1934 LaSalle convertible coupe, the sportiest vision of the marque.

Willoughby's undated proposal is fascinating, because this was a coachbuilder who primarily built enclosed bodies for Lincoln. The company's concentration on quantity series custom bodies suggests this model was not to be too limited an edition.

The owner of this 1934 Auburn six cylinder convertible sedan watches as her car receives special treatment while getting gas at this Baltimore, Maryland, service station.

The Pierce-Arrow exhibit at the 1935 Los Angeles automobile show included a club sedan trimmed to 1920s specifications with whitewall tires and two-tone paint.

Derham made these convertible sedan (above) and town car (opposite) proposals for Pierce-Arrow in 1935. Neither is known to have been built that year, but the town car body was put onto a 1936 Pierce chassis and survives today.

Pierce Arrow Town Car
The Derham Custom Body Co
Rosemont, Pa
1433

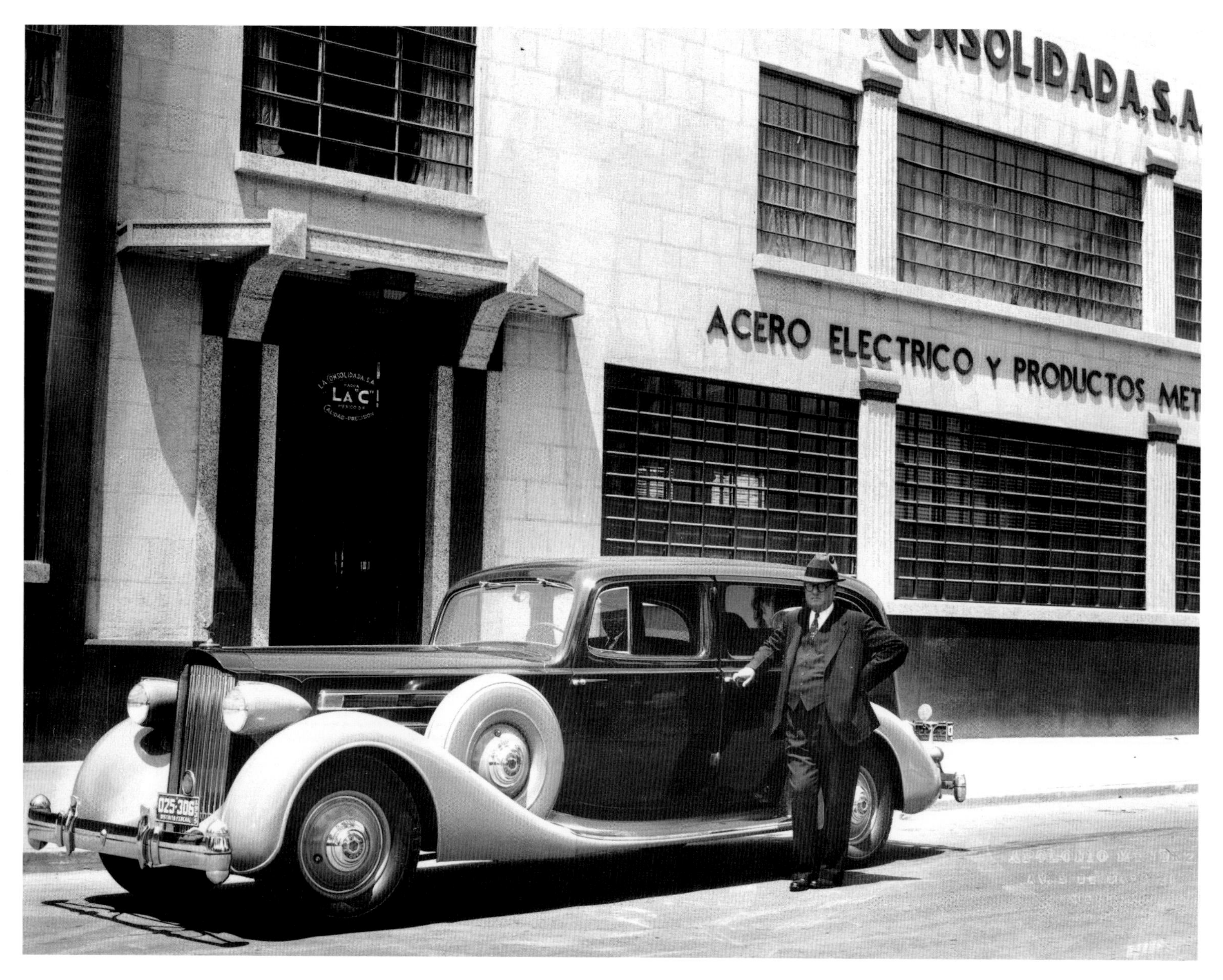

Packard redesigned its entire line of cars for 1935. This 1935 Packard model 1208 limousine had a 175 HP twelve cylinder engine on a 144-inch wheelbase chassis. It is visually interesting for its special two-tone paint, a feature not often seen in the mid-1930s.

The setting of the photograph is a manufacturing plant in Mexico City.

(opposite) An eight cylinder sedan makes a striking scene at the construction site of Hoover Dam in Nevada.

CALIFORNIA

Identical LeBaron series custom coupe bodies were available on 1935 (above) and 1936 (opposite) Lincoln KB chassis. The body adapted equally well to each year's different fender and radiator/front lines.

3330

When motion picture star Jean Arthur was making *Mr. Deeds Goes To Town*, an Auburn speedster provided the perfect accompaniment for the publicity photographs.

A 1936 supercharged Auburn convertible coupe has been bundled up against the cold winter in Lucerne, Switzerland.

The first production Cord 810 off the assembly lines was this sedan in February 1936. Two Auburn sedans of the same year symbolically face in the opposite direction.

The Cord 810 was the last significant new automobile produced by an independent manufacturer before World War II. But no matter how good it looked, it had not been perfected mechanically. Transmission problems plagued the first cars long enough to keep them from catching on.

The 810 was built on a relatively modest 125-inch wheelbase powered by a Lycoming-built 125 HP V-8 engine of 289 cubic inches.

J-54729

The secret of the Cord 810's breathtaking design was simplicity—dictated by a very tight budget, said to be under $1,000,000. This was a small amount to create an entire line of cars, even then.

Details of the car's body reveal a great deal of ingenuity. For example, the hubcaps were an off-the-shelf style with holes drilled not for appearance, but to allow heat to escape from the brakes.

A Packard convertible waits at the Greenbrier Hotel airport while William K. Vanderbilt's plane is made ready.

Cunningham's retreat to coachbuilding town car and limousine bodies on Ford chassis produced charming models such as this 1936 "enclosed drive town sedan."

In a "Motors" article in *The New Yorker* magazine, Speed (pen name for automotive writer G. F. T. Ryall) gave the car a great review, introducing the reader not only to the car but also to the showroom and its manager (John Dale at 253 West 64th Street in Manhattan). There was great appreciation of the coachbuilder's craft in the article. The restrained body lines, a "relief" from streamlining, were built of aluminum and ash wood framing with moldings rolled in the metal. "The paint job is extra special," added Speed. Technical comment applauded Cunningham for adding extra insulation to the body but suggested a change in shock absorbers would be in order.

This LaGrande-bodied Duesenberg phaeton is an excellent example of later Duesenbergs, which kept their early 1930s classic shape.

Pierce-Arrow was so short of money when introducing its 1937 models that it could only show its "New Special Five-Passenger Sedan" by retouching out the chauffeur's partition in this photo of a limousine on a 144-inch wheelbase. Building the car would have been almost as simple, replacing the partition and its jump seats with a sedan's front seat.

The angle at which Baltimore, Maryland, photographer A. Aubrey Bodine shot this 1937 Cord supercharged convertible adds to the charisma of the car.

Bodine was one of the principal photographers for the *Baltimore Sun* newspapers from the late-1920s until his death in 1970. His work was distinguished by an expressive printing process: there is often an aura in his finished prints not usually visible in his negatives.

Automotive interiors of the late-1930s are often as interesting as the cars' exteriors. The dash of this 1937 Cadillac sedan (above) is an intriguing mix of shapes and differently textured surfaces.

(opposite) A contrast is the LeBaron custom-bodied Lincoln Zephyr convertible sedan. It is a magnificent contemporary design of wood, leather, fabric, and chrome.

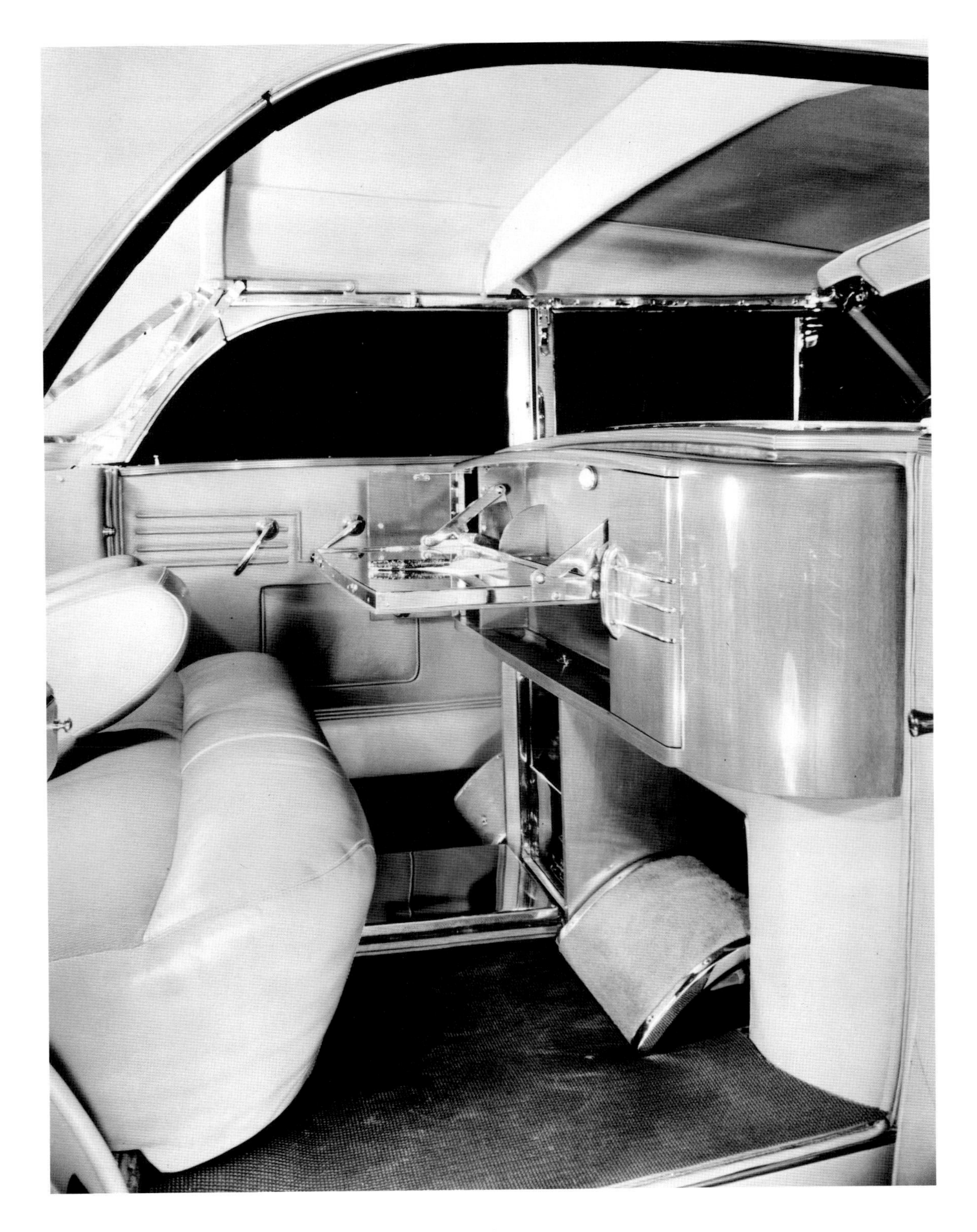

One of Pierce-Arrow's 1937 models was this formal sedan, a factory-built limousine body without a rear quarter window and a leather-covered roof, built on the long 147-inch wheelbase.

3S 533
19 CALIFORNIA 38

Derham built a series of ten convertible victorias on the Chrysler Imperial chassis from 1937 to 1939. This is the 1938 version.

DERHAM
ROSEMONT, PA

CHRYSLER IMPERIAL LIMOUSINE

Derham proposed this striking limousine body on a 1938 Chrysler Imperial chassis for New York City's mayor Fiorello LaGuardia. Political considerations probably would have kept this car from being built (at least with such conspicuous trim), but LaGuardia's predecessor, Jimmy Walker, might have enjoyed riding in it.

When President and Mrs. Roosevelt visited Yellowstone Park on December 13, 1937, they rode in a Cadillac convertible sedan. Following are Packard and Pierce-Arrow touring cars.

The chrome trim of the Cadillac stands out—the coordinated gleam of the hubcaps, molding, door handles, and window frames.

Just before the recession of 1938 forced Willoughby to close its doors, it proposed a berline landaulet for one of Don Lee's Cadillac customers. Cadillacs of this period with non-Fleetwood coachwork were extremely rare. It is not known if this car was ever built.

Probably the very last coachbuilder-bodied Pierce-Arrow was this 1938 Rollston observation sedan created for Henry B. Van Sinderen, a New York metals importer and exporter. One of the car's unusuai features is the rear seat facing away from the driver. The car was painted Buckingham gray with red pinstriping and a red leather interior.

The car is shown in front of the Congregational church in Washington, Connecticut, the site of Van Sinderen's country home. The car was driven a great deal—commuting from the city on the weekends and going out West every summer with a full complement of four passengers.

This 1938 Chrysler Imperial, with a special English-built Eyston body taking inspiration from Pierce's Silver Arrow, was one of the stars of London's annual Earl's Court automobile show.

One of the car's unusual interior features was its dashboard. The speedometer was lit in three colors depending on the car's speed: green up to 30 MPH, amber to 50 MPH, and red above 50 MPH.

LeBaron specially bodied a convertible touring car on the Lincoln K chassis for King George VI and Queen Elizabeth's 1939 tour of Canada and the United States. Here the car is in a parade in Victoria, British Columbia.

The car, which survives today, is a masterpiece in subtle uses of color. The maroon body is set off by a striking red pinstripe running along the side of the car. Wide whitewall tires highlight the hubcaps, finished in a bright blue enamel inset with a chrome symbol. The interior is a pale blue cloth.

This 1939 Hayes-bodied Chrysler coupe has just enough coachbuilder-type details, such as the side window moldings and rear end treatment, to give it a special look.

V 2007
19 MICH 39

One of the last attempts to revive interest in series custom coachwork was the younger Hermann Brunn's touring cabriolet, featuring a special window above the windshield.

First built for the 1937 model year, this particular body is on a 1939 Lincoln K 145-inch wheelbase chassis. Modestly popular at first—some two dozen were built in 1937 and 1938—only a handful were made in 1939. Others were built on Packard chassis. A proposal to include it in Pierce-Arrow's line never materialized.

The Lincoln Zephyrs at the top of the photograph contrast with the size of the touring cabriolet.

Edsel Ford's interest in good design made his personal cars quite special. But all pale beside his customized Lincoln Zephyr convertible victoria that was subsequently modified for production as the Lincoln Continental. Here, the original car, painted Ford's favorite gray, awaits shipment by truck to Ford's winter home in Hobe Sound, Florida, in February 1939.

22
MICH.
MANUFACTURER
39

"Oh God, not that again," exclaimed Lincoln's plant superintendent, when told Edsel Ford wanted a second Continental prototype. But by August 1939, the pre-production model was complete and production readied for the 1940 model year.

The designer, Eugene "Bob" Gregorie, recalled working on the car in an oral history for the Henry Ford Museum in 1985. He steadfastly maintained that the total design effort took no longer than one hour: primarily moving the Zephyr windshield back to lengthen the hood (which was also lowered) and adding a rear-mounted spare tire because the trunk was too small for a spare. There was no trim added because there was no tooling for trim on hand. The commercial advantage of the car was that it could be built with existing parts and materials.

22
MANUFACTURER
MICH
72967

Coachbuilder Howard "Dutch" Darrin had returned to the United States from France in the late-1930s and set up shop in Hollywood, California. His best known work was modifying a production Packard Super Eight into a smart convertible victoria. The first cars were built in Hollywood, but as demand increased, production was moved near the Packard plant in Detroit. Later, a small production line was operating in the old Auburn/Cord plant in Connersville, Indiana.

This is the 1939 model photographed on Belle Isle, Detroit.

This 1940 Packard was photographed on December 14, 1939, as part of Baltimore dealer Zell Motor Company's promotion with Esso gasoline.

Chrysler's mechanical and design leaps forward culminated in their 1940 LeBaron-bodied Thunderbolt coupe. The retractable top and 1950s style body suggest a Hollywood dream car, an interesting comparison with the Darrin Packards and Lincoln Continentals of the same year.

Towards the end of the Depression, the Farm Security Administration underwrote a number of photo shoots. Luxury automobiles in the city were probably not among the intended subjects, but the photographers noticed them and recorded some of what they saw.

In July 1941 photographer Jack Delano found a policeman giving directions at Washington's National Airport to the driver of this Buick Series 90 Roadmaster.

(opposite) A May 1943 launching party at the Bethlehem-Fairfield shipyards in Baltimore brought out this fleet of Packards. Standard production model limousines (with the split rear window) vie for attention among LeBaron-inspired models (with single-piece rear window) and a lone Clipper close-coupled sedan.

123-800
F28-017
194-266

Bibliography

"Advertising To Be Doubled By Cadillac." *San Francisco Chronicle*, November 15, 1936.

American Auto Appraisal. The American Reference and Appraisal Bureau. September, October, November, 1931.

"Another Buyer Selects Car Of Tomorrow." *The Pierce-Arrow News*, September 2, 1933.

"Anthony Takes Hudson Agency." *Los Angeles Examiner*, June 22, 1932.

"Anthony To Be Honored On Half Century Services." *Los Angeles Examiner*, February 28, 1954.

"Auburn Auto Files Plan." *New York Times*, July 29, 1939.

"Auto Dealer Succumbs To Heart Attack." *Los Angeles Examiner*, August 31, 1934.

"Automobile Exchange." *New York Times*, September 7, 1934.

Automotive Daily News, various issues 1931, 1932, 1934, 1935, 1936, 1938.

"Auto Salon Conducted At Biltmore." *Los Angeles Times*, February 14, 1932.

"Auto Salon Opens; 90 Models Shown." *New York Times*, December 2, 1930.

"Autos Open Year Of Showmanship." *Business Week*, October 30, 1937.

"A Year Later." *Fortune*, March 1932.

Ball, Thomas. Letter to Francis I. duPont, February 27, 1931.

Barnett, Lincoln. "Motors And Motoring." *The New Yorker*, October 25, 1941.

Barnett, Lincoln. "The Automobile Show." *The New Yorker*, October 12, 1940.

Blond, Stuart R. "The Duke of Earle." *The Packard Cormorant*, Spring and Summer 1985.

Brunn, Hermann A. Letter to Edsel Ford, May 9, 1932.

"Cadillac Records New Achievements." *Automobile Topics*, December 30, 1933.

Carson, Richard Burns. *The Olympian Cars*. New York: Alfred A. Knopf, 1976.

"Chrysler." *The Times*, October 18, 1938.

"Chrysler's Airflow Car Spectacular Offering." *Automobile Topics*, December 30, 1933.

City Directory—Baltimore, Maryland. R. L. Polk, 1933 and 1934.

City Directory—Detroit, Michigan. R. L. Polk, 1931 and 1932.

City Directory—San Francisco, California. R. L. Polk, 1933, 1934, and 1935.

"Cock of 1933." *Time*, January 8, 1934.

"Conkey P. Whitehead." *New York Times*, November 3, 1940.

"Cord Corp. May Change Name." *Business Week*, August 14, 1937.

Cuddy, G. A. Letter to National Automobile Chamber of Commerce, February 20, 1934.

"Custom And Challenger Models In New Stutz Line For Next Year." *New York Times*, December 30, 1934.

"Don Lee Daughters Given $300,000 In Estate Pact." *Los Angeles Examiner*, July 11, 1951.

"Don Lee Signs $8,000,000 Car Contract Here." *Los Angeles Examiner*, January 14, 1934.

Dunham, S. Roberts. "The Waterhouse Story." *The Classic Car*, September 1969.

duPont, E. Paul. Letter to A. J. Miranda, Jr., March 12, 1931.

duPont, E. Paul. Letter to Earl W. MacQuivey, February 7, 1933.

Economic and Trade Notes, United States Department of Commerce, various issues 1930–1938.

"Edward C. Worden, Chemist..." *New York Times*, September 23, 1940.

Elbert, J. L. *Duesenberg*. Post-Era Books, 1952.

"E. L. Cord Interests To Be Sold Today." *New York Times*, August 6, 1937.

Ema, Randy. "Duesenberg, Chariot Of The Gods." *Automobile Quarterly*, Volume 30, No. 4.

"Europe Copies Cord Designs." *San Francisco Chronicle*, February 1, 1932.

"Faulkner Again Heads Auburn Company Spurring Reports Of Cord Auto Merger." *New York Times*, August 25, 1934.

"Faulkner Tells How Auburn Did It." *Automobile Topics*, November 28, 1931.

Ford, Edsel. Letter to Hermann A. Brunn, May 3, 1932.

"Ford, Willys And Pierce Ready For New York Show." *Automotive Daily News*, November 11, 1936.

"4 Get Prison Terms In Securities Case." *New York Times*, September 7, 1937.

"Franklin Shatters Inter-City Record." *Miami Herald*, March 5, 1930.

"Franklin Shows Olympic Model." *Los Angeles Times*, January 8, 1933.

General Profit And Loss Statement. Pierce-Arrow Motor Car Company, December 31, 1932.

Grayson, Stan. "The Twelve At The End Of The Road." *Automobile Quarterly*. Third Quarter, 1979.

Gregorie, Eugene T. *Oral History*. Henry Ford Museum and Greenfield Village, 1989.

"Here Come The Cars." *Business Week*, December 9, 1933.

"High Hat Figures In Suit." *New York Times*, January 10, 1939.

Hildebrand, George. *The Golden Age Of The Luxury Car*. Dover, 1980.

"Jack Maddux Succumbs." *Los Angeles Times*, July 27, 1937.

"John Luther Maddux." *Automobile Topics*, August 2, 1937.

Kimes, Beverly Rae. *Packard*. Automobile Quarterly Publications, 1978.

Kimes, Beverly Rae and Clark, Henry Austin, Jr. *Standard Catalog Of American Cars 1805–1942*. Krause Publications,1989.

"Late Models And Styles Of Bodies Introduced By Heinrich Glaser, Dresden." *Autobody Trimmer And Painter*, July 1, 1931.

Lee, Don. "If I Were Broke What?" *Los Angeles Examiner*, April 18, 1928.

"Manning Heads Cord Corp. In New Set-Up." *Automobile Topics*, August 16, 1937.

"Marmon." *The Times*, October 22, 1931.

McHugh, F. D. "Motor Cars For 1934." *Scientific American*, February 1934.

"Michigan's Bank Holiday." *Literary Digest*, February 25, 1933.

"Michigan's Grim Holiday." *Business Week*, February 22, 1933.

Miranda, A. J., Jr. Letter to E. Paul duPont, December 15, 1930.

Miranda, A. J., Jr. Memo to the directors and shareholders of A. J. Miranda, Jr., Inc. Undated.

Mitchell, William L. *Reminiscences*. Henry Ford Museum and Greenfield Village, 1984.

Moody's Manual of Investments, 1936.

"Moon On The Motors." *Time*, September 3, 1934.

"Murphy, Car Dealer, Asks Bankruptcy." *Los Angeles Examiner*, March 10, 1933.

"Named Stutz Chief Engineer." *New York Times*, March 17, 1935.

"New Autos Follow Paris Gown Designs." *New York Times*, December 2, 1930.

"1940 Cars In Beauty Contest." *Business Week*, September 9, 1939.

"1937 Chryslers Were Designed By Lady Mendl." *Automotive Daily News*, November 7, 1936.

"NRA Rulings Spur New Auto Merger." *New York Times*, September 7, 1934.

Onativia, Elizabeth. "Salon Impresses Visitor." *New York Times*, December 7, 1930.

"Packard." *Fortune*, January 1937.

"Peerless Motor Cutting Surplus." *New York Times*, April 10, 1932.

"Pierce-Arrow Chief In S. F." *San Francisco Chronicle*, November 3, 1935.

Pinkson, Leon J. "Fine Auto Salon Opens At Palace." *San Francisco Chronicle*, February 28, 1932.

Prescott, Joel. "The Darrin Enigma." *The Classic Car*, March 1991.

Production Records. duPont Motors Incorporated, 1920–1932.

"Project Most Sensible One." *Los Angeles Examiner*, June 16, 1931.

"Ralph Hamlin Appointed Southern California Distributor." *Los Angeles Times*, April 9, 1933.

Regitko, Martin. "Willoughby." *The Classic Car*, Winter 1961.

"Reo Exhibits Custom Built Cars At Show." *San Francisco Chronicle*, February 1, 1931.

Roberts, Ralph. Letter to Edsel Ford, March 24, 1932.

Roe, Fred. *Duesenberg*. Dalton Watson, 1986.

Russell, Frederick C. "New Cars For '34 Give Motor World Epic Of Progress." *Motor Land*, January 1934.

"Salon de l'Automobile." *Vu*, October 1933.

Scurr, Isabel. Letter to L. F. Hostly, November 3, 1930.

"Small Car de Luxe." *Business Week*, March 31, 1934.

Speed (G. F. T. Ryall). "Motors." *The New Yorker*, November 22, 1930; December 12, 1931; May 14, 1932; September 14, 1935; and November 22, 1936.

Speed (G. F. T. Ryall). "Motors and Motoring." *The New Yorker*, October 15, 1938 and September 30, 1939.

Speed (G. F. T. Ryall). "The Automobile Show." *The New Yorker*, January 6, 1934 and October 14, 1939.

Starr, Kevin. *Material Dreams*. Oxford, 1990.

Stevens, Otheman. "Murphy Motor Rooms Social Center For Day." *Los Angeles Examiner*, January 16, 1930.

Stout, Richard H. "The Proposed Lincoln For 1940." *The Classic Car*, June 1992.

"Striking Progress In 1933 Cars." *Scientific American*, January 1933.

"Studebaker Comes Back." *Fortune*, February 1935.

"Stutz Increases Prices." *New York Times*, March 26, 1930.

"Stutz Plans For RFC Loan." *New York Times*, January 17, 1935.

Sutton, George W., Jr. "Buyers of Motor Luxury," *The American Automobile* (overseas edition), October 1931.

"The Lady And The Topper." *New York Times*, January 11, 1939.

"To Buy Marmon Plant." *New York Times*, January 10, 1934.

"21 Angelenos Insured For Million Plus." *Los Angeles Examiner*, September 25, 1930.

"Veteran Auto Executive Takes Over Branch Unit." *Los Angeles Times*, February 29, 1931.

Vienne, Veronique. "In A Class By Themselves." *Town & Country*, November 1994.

"Will Buy Franklin Plant." *New York Times*, March 10, 1936.

Willoughby, Francis D. Letter to Mr. Rowsome, January 9, 1933.

Witteried, J. E. "Concours d'Elegance de l'Auto; Parc des Princes." *Autobody Trimmer and Painter*, September 1931.

Zim, Larry; Lerner, Mel; and Rolfes, Herbert. *The World Of Tomorrow*. Harper & Row, 1988.

Credits

Pages 42, 45, 66, and 115 are courtesy of the American Automobile Manufacturers' Association.

Pages 80, 84, 85 are courtesy of the Auburn-Cord-Duesenberg Museum.

Pages 43, 109 are courtesy of the *Automobil Revue*.

Pages 44, 89 are courtesy of the Automobile Hall of Fame.

Pages 71, 81, 116, 117 are courtesy of the Bass Photo Co., Indiana Historical Society.

Pages 70, 88, 122, and 123 are courtesy of the Behring Museum.

Page 3 courtesy of the Bettmann Archive.

Page 131 is courtesy of the British Columbia Archives and Records Service.

Pages 76, 77, 132, 133, 142, and 143 are courtesy of the Chrysler Historical Collection.

Pages 102, 103, 124, and 125 are courtesy of the Classic Car Club of America—Noel Thompson Library.

Page 54 is courtesy of John Conde.

Pages 50 and 51 are courtesy of Bill Creteur.

Pages 92 and 93 are courtesy of the Ford Motor Company.

Pages 44, 72, 106, 107, 110, 111, 112, 113, and 130 are courtesy of the Free Public Library of Philadelphia.

Pages 21, 48, 49, 53, 91, 98, 120, 121, 128, 134, 135, 136, 137, 138, and 139 are courtesy of the Henry Ford Museum and Greenfield Village.

Pages 64 and 90 are courtesy of Tom Hubbard.

Pages 9, 52, 67, 96, 97, and 105 are courtesy of the Huntington Library, San Marino, California.

Pages 94 and 95 are courtesy of LeSoir (Rossel & Cie.).

Pages 126, 127, 144, 145 are courtesy of the Library of Congress.

Page 6 is courtesy of Moulin Studios.

Pages 59, 86, and 87 are courtesy of the National Archives.

Pages 74, 104, and 140 are courtesy of the National Automotive History Collection, Detroit Public Library.

Pages 62 and 63 are courtesy of the National Motor Museum—Beaulieu.

Pages ii, vi, viii, 45, 55, 56, 65, 78, and 79 are courtesy of the Oakland Museum.

Pages 40, 57, 68, 69, 73, 75, 100, 119, and 141 are courtesy of the Peale Museum, Baltimore City Life Museums.

The cover and page 118 are courtesy of the Pierce-Arrow Collection, Special Collections Library, University of Michigan.

Pages 46, 47, and 99 are courtesy of the Romer Collection, Miami-Dade Public Library.

Pages 60, 61, and 114 are courtesy of the Greenbrier.

Page 129 is courtesy of Thomas T. Solley.

Pages 28, 94, and 95 are courtesy of the Studebaker National Museum.

Page 3 is courtesy of the Hearst Collection, *Los Angeles Examiner*, Department of Special Collections, University of Southern California Library.

Page 101 is courtesy of the Vogue Tyre and Rubber Company.

Page 58 is courtesy of the Western Reserve Historical Society.

Page 108 is courtesy of the William F. Harrah Foundation National Automobile Museum research archives.

Pages 82 and 83 are courtesy of Waite W. Worden.

Index

ABOUT THE TYPE

The text and displays are set in several sizes of Gill Sans, a sans serif typeface designed in 1928 by the British artist Eric Gill. The subtle shapes in the strokes of Gill Sans letters create an especially attractive look that is part of the 1930s era.